ADVANCE PRAISE

This is a highly readable and actionable book on Turnaround management. In a disruptive scenario, practically every business faces crisis one time or the other and this book will sensitise you about the challenges, doable action plan and strategies. The book by someone who has undertaken turnaround of HMV as CEO and has advised many companies is 24 carat gold which every entrepreneur big or small should keep on his bookshelf.

—Dr Anil K. Khandelwal, Former Chairman Bank of Baroda and author of the bestselling 'Dare to Lead'

Leading a business in today's dynamic environment is hard enough, but turning around a sick and almost bankrupt company seems impossible. Even the best run companies face these difficult situations as technology and consumer preferences change. In this book Pradip Chanda has distilled years of personal experience into powerful lessons for leading such a turnaround. Every senior business leader would benefit from reading this book.

—Sunil Gupta, Edward W. Carter Professor of Business, Harvard Business School

This book is very different from whatever you might have ever read about a turnaround. Coming from first hand experiences of the author with a narrative that touches one's core, makes it a must read. Whether your company is facing a turnaround situation, a near crisis or any challenges common to any organisation, you will draw several lessons and eye popping insights.

—Rajiv Gupta, VP Marketing & Strategy, Honda Cars India and Alumnus, Harvard Business School

In Utilizing Hidden Assets, we have a practical handbook for turning around a failing company by identifying and exploiting unrecognized assets. Combining his own experience with extensive knowledge, Chanda provides step-by-step directions for developing an immediate strategy, using 'hidden' assets to support it, and implementing within the constraints of tight resources. Though addressed to turnaround, the insights of this book should be of use to any CEO.

—Ellen Weisbord, Ph.D., Professor of Management, Academic Director, Executive MBA Program Lubin School of Business, Pace University

Mr. Pradip Chanda offers in this book, an immediately implementable set of action ideas for Business Turnaround. He is extremely well equipped to do this out of the painful, direct, personal experience of leading a turnaround. He went from a Marketing background, in a MNC, to an Indian family conglomerate. To his credit, faced with a turnaround situation, he quickly picked up the essential finance, HR, change management and leadership competences. The first few pages of Chapter 1, where he dramatically portrays the imaginary conversation between a CEO and his CXO's in a turnaround crisis, attest to his direct experience of the trauma and the ways out of it.

—Dr Mrityunjay Athreya, Padma Bhushan

RISE LIKE A
PHOENIX

RISE LIKE A PHOENIX

SCRIPTING CORPORATE TURNAROUND

PRADIP CHANDA

Los Angeles | London | New Delhi
Singapore | Washington DC | Melbourne

First published in 2017 by

SAGE Publications India Pvt Ltd
B1/I-1 Mohan Cooperative Industrial Area
Mathura Road, New Delhi 110 044, India
www.sagepub.in

SAGE Publications Inc
2455 Teller Road
Thousand Oaks, California 91320, USA

SAGE Publications Ltd
1 Oliver's Yard, 55 City Road
London EC1Y 1SP, United Kingdom

SAGE Publications Asia-Pacific Pte Ltd
3 Church Street
#10-04 Samsung Hub
Singapore 049483

Published by Vivek Mehra for SAGE Publications India Pvt. Ltd, typeset in 11/13 pts Berkeley by Zaza Eunice, Hosur, Tamil Nadu, India and printed at Chaman Enterprises, New Delhi.

Library of Congress Cataloging-in-Publication Data Available

ISBN: 978-93-860-6242-0 (PB)

SAGE Team: Sachin Sharma, Priya Arora, Madhurima Thapa and Ritu Chopra

To my grandchildren, Tara, Maile and Palmer
who seem to be as committed to reuse, recycle and renew as I am

Bulk Sales

SAGE India offers special discounts
for purchase of books in bulk.
We also make available special imprints
and excerpts from our books on demand.

For orders and enquiries, write to us at

Marketing Department
SAGE Publications India Pvt Ltd
B1/I-1, Mohan Cooperative Industrial Area
Mathura Road, Post Bag 7
New Delhi 110044, India

E-mail us at **marketing@sagepub.in**

Get to know more about SAGE

Be invited to SAGE events, get on our mailing list.
Write today to **marketing@sagepub.in**

This book is also available as an e-book.

CONTENTS

PREFACE

The signs of stress in a company often begin as ripples in nooks and crannies below the senior management's radars. Small dealers resign. The stock to turnover ratio on retail shelves increase. Order books shrink. Unsold inventories rise.

Alarm bells start ringing when the market share charts keep going south, sales drop and the cash inflows become tighter. Knee jerk reactions follow. Data-based, reasoned decision-making becomes the first casualty. Deep discounting destroys carefully nurtured brand positioning. Costs are indiscriminately cut, processes suffer, quality issues multiply and customers cancel orders. Jobs are threatened, good people resign and others begin looking for jobs. Demoralization sets in at all levels.

Disruption, which everybody has been talking about, seems to have caught the company with its pants down.

The urge to invite strategy consultants to chart out paths for restructuring, revitalizing, renewing or reinventing the company, whatever you may want to call it, becomes strong. The consultants will focus on strategy reformulation and prescribe a silver bullet to cure all. Most of these solutions are resource hungry.

A cash-strapped demoralized organization is rarely ready to fire the silver bullet, no matter how potent it sounds.

Such a company has to first go through a painful turnaround process to restabilize and prepare to launch a renewal programme.

It has to find resources from within, find innovative uses of existing (often neglected) assets, use cost management as a strategic tool to enhance competitiveness, embark on short-term strategic initiatives to revive the company's morale and confidence and formulate a viable and sustainable business model.

This book is about managing the turnaround process. The C-Suite of companies faced with possible turnaround challenges may find this book useful and practical, primarily because it draws on the author's own experience and other case studies, both real and hypothetical, to expand on four key components of a turnaround framework—asset utilization, cost management, renewal and rethinking business model.

My first book on asset utilization based turnaround strategies was published way back in 2000. The market place has changed, but amazingly some of the principles of turnaround management discussed in that book have remained relevant even now, as highlighted in more recent case studies. I seek the reader's forgiveness for reproducing the HMV case study from the previous book, because it is one of the better asset utilization-based successful turnaround cases that I know of.

Pradip Chanda
June, 2016
pradipchanda@outlook.com

ACKNOWLEDGEMENTS

Interactions with hundreds of business executives, consultants, academics and colleagues in the 40+ years, as a practicing manager and a consultant, have helped me greatly in gaining insights into the challenges companies face as they go through their life cycles and how managers respond to them. I thank them all.

Being a reasonably avid reader of all genres of books, including those by eminent management thinkers, I must acknowledge their influence on my thinking and writing style, and thank them too. There are a few specific quotes from some of the books/articles I have read, and I have acknowledged the source and the author in the text.

There are also excerpts from public sources of information like annual reports of companies, websites, newspapers and magazines, and the sources have been acknowledged in relevant chapters.

Professor Sunil Gupta, a onetime colleague and a good friend, has been a constructive critic and the structure of the book reflects his valuable inputs.

My sons, Pramit and Pratik have been the usual pillars of support and I thank them for being there when I needed help in research and formatting the book.

Finally, thank you to Sachin Sharma of SAGE Publications, for his enthusiastic support.

CHAPTER 1

THE CHALLENGE OF TURNAROUNDS
A DAY IN THE LIFE OF A TURNAROUND CEO

*B*elieve it or not, most turnaround chief executive officers (CEOs) and C-Suite managers' day may begin with a meeting among the head honchos of Finance, Supply Chain, Manufacturing and Marketing to get a consensus on how today's trickle of available cash should be spent.

Director Finance will begin by tabling a report on yesterday's collections and the closing bank balance. He will then produce a long list of 'must pay now' items, all of which are non-revenue generating.

Director Marketing will produce a list of long pending customer orders and demand that factories produce these by the end of the day.

Director Manufacturing will say that it will be tool downtime in 2 hours as no supplies of raw materials have come in yesterday. That apart unless some spares reach the factory by sundown some of the machines will lie idle even if raw materials come in plenty.

Director Supply Chain will say that no vendor is answering his calls and unless he gets a few bank drafts on hand he cannot get any trucks to move from any supplier.

What would you do?

As the meeting winds down, the Finance Director requests a few minutes of private time with the CEO. In a voice filled with gravitas appropriate for his position, he again warns the CEO of the dangers of not releasing some overdue interest payments to the lead banks. He then winks and asks whether he can get the Board's approval to open an account in a private bank outside the lending consortium and put all deposits there. Why? This way the consortium banks will not be able to deduct interest payments from the deposits! The CEO likes his lateral thinking.

Next, the Marketing Director pops his head in for his private chat. Look, he says, let me be candid. I am asking my reps to stop calling on customers.

Why on earth would you do that?

These guys are upset. They can't take abuse from the customers any more for not delivering on past orders.

Really, all of them have a long list of pending orders?

Not all, the Marketing Director agrees, but the star rep does and he is the leader.

And, the CEO says, 'He is not getting his commissions either on unfulfilled orders, right?' Exactly, says the Marketing Director, you already know what the problem is.

The CEO having found out that the star rep's clients' bills are overdue, is able to say to the Marketing Director, 'You know about our cash flow issues; instead of getting your guys to collect you are happy to sit back and let one disgruntled rep disrupt our business process? Have you explained our predicament to our clients and asked them for co-operation to tide us over the present problem? I suggest you start making client visits immediately' and packs him off.

The Supply Chain Director knocks and enters. Can I be candid too?

Why not, says the CEO, we are in this mess together.

Exactly, says SC. I had promised all my suppliers that all their old dues will be cleared as soon as the new CEO comes on board.

You did, why?

I assumed that you would have known our cash flow position before you joined and would have arranged for fresh fund inflow from the promoters.

Well, says the new CEO, I did know the cash flow position. But I also figured out that if the promoters had the funds floating around, we wouldn't have got into such a jam. You should have known that too, and not made promises we can't keep. As it is, our credibility with your suppliers must be low, stretching it further will only make matters worse.

But, continues the CEO, I hear you are in conversation with a consortium of suppliers about settling a part of their past dues as you settle their bills for fresh supplies. This is a great initiative. Would you like me to attend a meeting or two with you to lend you some moral support?

Yes, please, says SC and trots off to set up a suppliers meet.

The Manufacturing Director comes in to casually say Bye.

How do you mean?

I am done.

Done?

Yes, done. I can't stand this sniggering from the workers any more. Day in and day out no raw materials, no spares, only loads of free time.

Tough, says the CEO. But I must compliment you on computerizing your inventories recently. I was looking at some printouts. The spares inventory list seems to be very long. Are all these round pegs for square holes? How on earth were these ordered? Can't they be used?

Couple of minutes' silence follows.

Then the CEO says, I was reading some where the other day how a company managed to get 15 out of 20 machines working by temporarily cannibalizing parts from other machines, instead of letting all 20 sit idle. I am sure you have done that.

I also hear that lately quality complaints have gone up. You must have process quality norms in place. Idle time may be a good time to refresh worker memories about the processes and remind them about how critical it is to get it right the first time, when times are as rough as they are now.

This is a make-believe conversation, right? The words certainly are.

But the reality is that in all cash-strapped companies such conversations happen every day and often more than once.

How do such situations arise?

De-growth and stagnation begins when a company begins to lose control of its own destiny.

Markets change, consumer habits and attitudes change, new products often revolutionize how customer needs are met, new competitors aggressively play predatory price cards and e-tailers disrupt businesses through traditional channels. Many companies fail to realize the impact of these changes on their business model–product, positioning, price, customer profile et al. on time and make the cardinal error of hanging on to traditional business models and processes.

The results are inevitable, a slide down a tortuous path towards bankruptcy or sickness, as it is called in India.

Many operating managers working in well-managed companies may at times feel the tremors caused by a temporary loss of market share or reduced margins on some product lines when competition forces them to run a 'price off' or BOGOFF campaign. But few, if any, would have experienced the agony of continuous loss of market share, rapid and irreversible erosion of margins, severe cash flow crunches resulting in diminishing working capital, inability to pay suppliers and finally to service debts especially from banks and financial institutions. For such managers, a turnaround challenge would be a nightmare.

Norms vary from country to country, but failure to pay bank interests on time for two consecutive quarters is by and large the red flag used by most lenders to declare loans to such companies as non-performing assets and begin the loan recovery process. Bankruptcy laws are in place in most countries to aid and abet lenders to recover their doubtful loans.

Owners and managers of such under-performing companies often wake up to the need to mount a turnaround offensive only at this stage, and reach out to consulting companies. Consulting companies are actually very good in articulating strategies for transformation, restructuring and reinvention, and come up with a 'silver bullet', which fired from the right gun and aimed correctly will certainly turn the companies around.

Unfortunately, most companies at this stage are rarely in a position to use this bullet effectively, as the 'firing gun'—the company—is often in shambles by now and needs to get the launch pad ready first. This is the first and foremost challenge of a turnaround.

A sick company's personality is the first reality facing the turnaround manager.

Marketers attach great value to the concept of brand personality. If your cake of soap were a car would it be a Mercedes or a Hyundai? One small step forward, and if it were a person would she be Gisele Bündchen or the lady next door?

Companies also have personalities. These are really the manifestations of the company's culture. A buoyant company appears confident and sure in everything it does, and that rubs off on its people. Success seems to be destined for them.

Virgin is a good example. Its founder Sir Richard Branson has brought to bear his larger than life personality in all businesses he has launched and people have no trepidation in putting large sums of money upfront to reserve seats on his proposed space flights which have been on the drawing board for many years.

Under-performing companies on the other hand transmit their anxieties, built up over a period of sustained insecurities, in everything they do.

If you were to walk into one, you would probably expect to see rusty, unused machines in its plants, peeling walls and grubby patches in its offices.

What you will not be prepared for will be the expressions of the utterly defeated, on the faces of the employees. They seem to personify the company, a derelict waiting for its deliverance or, more probably, its doom.

To the turnaround manager, this internal personality crisis is the biggest challenge.

Damages which could have been caused by external threats have already happened. Competitors have taken the business away, facilities have become 'obsolete' and good people have been poached. The environment has become more threatening with global players offering better and cheaper products, more freely available in markets forced to lift cross-border trade restrictions.

If the company is to revive, a change in its personality is the starting point.

The first obstacle is the mindset of the middle managers and the office staff. They would be insecure and resist changes. Of greater concern would be their cynicism, their refusal to accept that a rescue is possible. This will manifest itself in infuriating responses—it cannot be done, that's not the way it works, we have tried it before.

Pushed into adopting new ways they will, at times involuntarily, gang up to make sure that things do not work. They will resist efficiencies—the fear of redundancy is real. They will attend training sessions under duress and the net takeout will be near zero. Gangs will form—some will be sycophantic, others siding with new management, through back biting and complaining against others. Only a very few will lend genuine support to the changes. They need to be spotted early, protected and nursed into change agents.

The CEO needs to be aware of these forces at work. He must have a plan to tackle this malaise. He has to trigger off a cultural metamorphosis that will reshape the mindsets. Good ideas, introduced too early, without changing the work culture, will be buried unceremoniously.

The human resource asset audit process must be realistic on this count. Too often, experience and expertise are negative assets without the right mindset.

The second cultural challenge lies in integrating the workforce into the mainstream. Workers, contrary to conventional management wisdom, are actually more attuned to work. They are familiar with accountability as their contribution is more easily measurable, even to themselves, and they feel more vulnerable if the company is doing badly. They see declining sales and mounting inventories for what they are—a lead up to fall in production—and disappearance of their jobs and income. They have seen too many closures, layoffs and lockouts not to believe that their livelihood is at stake.

It is natural therefore that they fall back on their own 'skill sets' for security. Efforts to retrain them to do jobs other than those based on their skills will cause concern, especially if the unit has various job classes that have historically determined a hierarchy. Breaking it down in an acceptable manner and getting the workers to branch out to new skills will do wonders to the whole company's mindset change.

How would a Turnaround Manager bring about a change in the personality? *Many would argue that unveiling a bold vision is the first step. Rousing town hall meetings urging everyone to pursue the new vision is a widely practiced opening gambit.* Writing a bold vision is not very difficult, in fact it is easy to lock oneself up in the office, google vision statements of the most admired companies and cobble together a grand statement. The question is: will it be credible? Isn't the battered organization too cynical to buy into a grand vision, when the everyday reality is that the company doesn't even have the wherewithal to feed the idle machines with raw material.

Should one not scale the vision down a little and talk about an achievable milestone in the short term as the only goal for now and get the organization to go for it?

Talking about the organization, the best talents have left you. Those remaining seem to be time servers, nowhere to go, not much direction coming from the top, loads of crib time.

Even if you had the money to pay market prices you will be hard pressed to get good managers to join a sick company. Masochists are not all that common in any society.

So what do you do?

Time and time again, you may have walked into various organizations, to speed post a letter, sort out a payment dispute at a telecom office or get some mistake in some record corrected and found the general work ethic subpar, to put it mildly. Even there, you must have found at least one or two people busy working, ignoring the jabbering around them and volunteering to resolve your problem. This should give the CEO faith in saying that even in the worst of times there will be some, perhaps a few second line managers who can be groomed to take on more responsibility, and more importantly be the change agents needed to bring in some fresh thinking and work culture.

The CEO's best bet will be to find them, hang on to them and motivate them to be a part of the turnaround initiative.

How and when?

The Burning Issue

Anything the new Turnaround Manager wants to do will require cash, a commodity often in acute short supply in a tough turnaround situation.

By default, the most important pressing question facing the Turnaround CEO is how do I mobilize resources meaning cash and from where? This question will hound the CEO every minute of his first few days and weeks as he sits through endless meetings, talking about 'no monies' and robs him of sleep at night.

If there is a will there is a way, so goes an old adage. Yes, one can actually find sources of cash hidden even in a sick company if only one looks at the assets with a fresh set of eyes. The balance sheet is a good place to start followed by an audit of the capabilities of the men and machines. Diligence will pay off. Some 'encashable' assets can always be found lying buried in the debris of a sick company.

A Recap

A Turnaround Manager's primary task is to transform a demoralized organization into a fighting unit ready to revitalize the company.

Resources will have to be found from within a careful audit of assets and innovative utilization of such assets is often the only option.

The renewal process begins with sharp focus on an immediate positive, preferably revenue multiplying activity involving as many people as possible.

Rethink and design a sustainable business model which makes the company viable again.

Difficult to achieve? No one will claim that it is easy. But it has been done and can be done again and again.

Let me take you down memory lane, in the next chapter, the HMV story, where I modestly explain what I did in a similar situation.

CHAPTER 2

DOWN MEMORY LANE
THE HMV STORY

Back in the 1980s, the Government of India had promulgated the Sick Industrial Companies (Special Provisions) Act, 1985 (SICA). Soon, thereafter, the Board for Industrial and Financial Reconstruction (BIFR) was set up as an agency of the Department of Financial Services of the Ministry of Finance to identify under-performing industrial companies heading towards closure, to be known henceforth as a sick company, and assist in reviving those that may be viable and shutting down the others.

A sick company was defined as one where the accumulated losses of the company, as at the end of any financial year have resulted in erosion of 50 per cent or more of its peak net worth during the immediately preceding four financial years. It became mandatory for the board of such companies to refer it to BIFR within six months of the end of the financial year and be officially notified as one.

By the time I joined Gramophone Company of India Ltd., better known as HMV, as the President and CEO towards the end of 1985, the company's accumulated losses had completely wiped out it's net worth. The company was about to earn the dubious distinction of being one of the earliest companies to be referred to BIF as a sick company as required by SICA.

The first task was obviously to figure out what went wrong with a company which was a household name in the country and had a virtual monopoly in the recorded music business for almost 80 years.

The Gramophone & Typewriter Company Ltd. pioneered recording of Indian artists for reproduction as phonographs when they set up their very first branch in India in 1902, barely two years after the incorporation the parent company in England. A roving team of sound recording engineers unearthed such an abundance of musical talent across the country that soon recording studios were set up in all major cities to create an as yet unmatched repertoire library of all genres of Indian music by well-known and promising vocal and instrumental artists.

The company then set up an exclusive dealer network in the then undivided India to promote HMV, (the parent brand) phonographs, 78 rpm shellac records played on hand-wound record players with a horn.

The demand far exceeded expectations, and when the 78 rpm records made way for the 45 and 33 rpm vinyl records, the company invested heavily on a factory to make 'enough' records. The 45 and 33 rpm records remained the norm for the industry for well over 40 years till the late 1970s.

Meanwhile HMV's popular repertoire got a major boost when silent films became talkies and HMV acquired the record rights of movie sound tracks.

To facilitate deeper penetration of records, the company had also set up a large unit to manufacture record players, which were sold at subsidized prices. This unit was self-contained, with a full-fledged, mechanized carpentry shop to make the bases, an engineering work shop to manufacture the springs, sound box and other mechanical components, a forge to make the horns and a print shop to print the record sleeves.

Arguably, a brilliant marketing move at the time, which turned out to be a millstone around the company's neck in the late 1970s which brought about disruptions on many fronts, none of which the local management could anticipate and/or prevent.

By the early 1970s, HMV was the primary repository of recorded Indian music as the company continued to build up a formidable repertoire of music from all parts of the country and of course it had access to international music from its parent company. HMV became virtually synonymous with the Indian music industry from its inception and retained over 90 per cent share of the market for well over 70 odd years. The fact that setting up a record pressing plant was capital intensive and therefore acted as a formidable entry barrier against small competitors, gave HMV an 'unfair' advantage to retain its market dominance.

Those were the halcyon days of analogue music.

Then technology changed. HMV's parent company EMI Music had a handful to deal with.

HMV India had other disruptions to contend with at the same time.

The first disruption was a piece of legislation which required HMV's British parent to divest 60 per cent of the shares to local investors. To exacerbate matters, a Left government was elected in West Bengal at around the same time, where the company's factory was located. The government's sympathy for the labour unions gave rise to violent militancy which led to a mass exodus of most manufacturing units from the state. Those who could not shift their business to other states became pawns in the hands of such unions. Both these extraneous factors made the parent company lose interest in the Indian market.

Then came *coup de grâce*. Music cassettes appeared on the scene and rapidly replaced records primarily because of its mobility. The company followed suit but had to fight an unscripted battle with both its hands tied behind its back.

When music cassettes appeared on the scene, it was obvious that setting up a music duplication facility using cassette-to-cassette duplicating machines required very little capital. The government in its wisdom, therefore, decided to reserve pre-recorded cassettes for the small scale sector. The fact that this sector neither had access to any music catalogue nor had the wherewithal to set up recording studios, completely eluded the mandarins.

The result was not unexpected. A number of 'entrepreneurs' decided that HMV's catalogue was fair game and should be used as 'masters'. The freebie was the master—the price of an HMV record, a few rupees versus substantial costs in recording, paying life-long royalties to artists and paying large advances to producers for film soundtrack rights. The price of pre-recorded cassettes plummeted.

To compound matters, HMV's production capacity was pegged at a meagre two and a half million cassettes a year. This was nowhere near the market demand and the pirates had a huge hole to fill profitably. The opportunity was so large that the biggest pirate soon put up multiple factories to make cassettes and even set up a magnetic tape manufacturing plant. He also created a parallel fly by night dealer network buying stocks from a few company appointed handpicked wholesalers, and literally selling pirated cassettes as roadside hawkers do, displaying their ware from baskets, trays and foldable display units, here today, somewhere else tomorrow.

The death knell began tolling by the early 1980s. HMV's market share remained at about 90 per cent of the legitimate music business, but, alas, the pirated cassettes outsold HMV's by a factor of 20 to 1, all blaring stolen music recorded by HMV at substantial cost, and unwittingly providing the 'master' for unscrupulous 'New Music Labels'. Its factory soon became a white elephant as most of the 3,000 odd employees had no work but downsizing was not an option, not in the militant environment.

The owners, EMI, caught in a Hobson's choice decided to bring in industry veterans as CEOs from other countries to work their way out of this mess. But the poor CEOs had no understanding of the Indian market, the laws, or rather the absence of any laws to protect copyrights, the fly by night dealer network selling pirated cassettes, connivance of local authorities with pirates to spread the menace, presumably for substantial considerations.

All that EMI could do was change CEOs.

The first CEO to fall was in 1978. The next in 1983. The one after him lasted till end 1985.

And then I walked in.

All companies expect changes from a new CEO. In a company doing well, the new CEO is able to focus on a somewhat longer horizon. Consequently, he can take some time to initiate major changes in the manner in which the business is run. He can also concentrate on building up competencies, incrementally or modularly, department by department or division by division as he unfolds his long-term goals. Most importantly, he is free from the pressures of a daily resource crunch that forces a constant juggling between what should be done and what can be done.

Under-achieving or sick companies need changes, and that too, on a war footing.

The CEO does not have the luxury of choosing the business either. The mandate is loud and clear—turn the company's present business around.

HMV was a classic basket case, if ever there was one.

Product and technology obsolescence, rampant piracy eroding its ability to protect its IP (intellectual property) in the easy to duplicate new format, music cassettes, grossly overmanned factory and offices, abysmally low productivity in a hostile environment with a left government and a militant union. The list of woes did not stop there.

The pirated cassettes had spawned a parallel distribution network, and the company sales force was unable to find an entry into this network. Even loyal dealers were switching to other businesses to stay alive.

Losses were escalating, creditors–banks and financial institutes were breathing down their necks, and to cap it all, the contracted artists were demanding long overdue royalties before recording new albums.

Vendors were reluctant to continue supplies, and raw material and component supplies were virtually hand to mouth, on some days not even that.

The owners, EMI Music, a British multi-national, must have been ecstatic when approached by a leading local industrialist, known as the takeover tycoon, to buy them out. It was a great escape from a no-win situation for them.

The new owner was aware of the pressure to keep HMV going. It was not just another business venture; it was an institution, a preserver of India's rich musical heritage, a nurturer of talent. The government, the unions, the creditors, the artists, the music loving public wouldn't let such an institution close.

Reviving the business, against all odds, was therefore my mandate.

What was obvious was that it would take a lot of time, effort and innovation to turn it around, because there were exposed flanks on every side. The total effort had to be multi-focus.

It would take time to persuade the unions to accept the need to rightsize, change productivity norms, close down units which were no longer relevant to the core business and could not be viable as separate businesses. These had to be demonstrated to the union to get their buy-in.

Simultaneously, the banks had to be cajoled to not only restructure loans, but give additional loans in the short term to cover working capital needs, fund a voluntary retirement scheme for the excess manpower, as and when the union agrees to accept a voluntary retirement scheme (VRS) for redundant employees.

The organization was in disarray. The previous CEO was sent on leave when the takeover happened, a couple of months before I came on board.

The organization was top heavy with eight vice-presidents (VPs), each operating within a silo, each convinced that having no working capital was the only problem the company was facing. There were no systems of management committee meetings or any forums for joint deliberations. Everyone seemed to wait for cash infusion following the takeover but no one seemed to have a plan for utilization of the much awaited cash, other than negotiating a golden handshake for himself.

There was no management information system and no data available to make informed decisions.

Investing in information analytics was a must before systems and procedures could be revived, and a dynamic marketing team needed to come on board to create products for those segments where piracy was low.

Capacity build up was not an issue. Capacity utilization combined with low-cost capability was the challenge. The company had enhanced its cassette production capacity to 10 million units per annum but had never produced more than 2,50,000 a month. Not enough orders in the pipeline.

Distribution strategies needed change, both to create 'pirate proof' channels as well as to reach out to the parallel retail network created by the pirates.

Artists had to be wooed back and the search for new talent needed to be reintroduced.

Piracy had to be fought, in the market place, in courtrooms and even in ministry corridors who drafted copyright protection laws. A single company cannot generate government sympathy. An industry body can. A moribund industry body existed. This needed to be revived.

The immediate concern was cash, especially as the residual funds available, after some not so well thought out expenditures in the first two months of the takeover, to me were a tiny fraction of what was required to do battle on all fronts. Waiting for a fresh inflow of funds would be futile as an equity-linked debenture public offer flopped miserably. As a result, I had to generate resources from within.

This left me with only one strategy option—unlock the value in the present assets. What I call the asset utilization strategy.

The First Priority

RENEWAL

The success of an asset utilization based strategy depends entirely on making the organization believe that there remains some inherent strength (assets) even when the company appears to be on the brink of collapse, and that diligence in utilizing such assets shall produce results. With luck, one such activity can be a pointer to a sustainable competitive advantage for the company to build upon and get moving on the road to recovery.

The first priority is to *embark on one or more revenue generating activities utilizing the company's remaining assets*, and not, I repeat not, generate revenue by selling assets. No revenue meant no salaries at the end of the month, and that was suicide in the climate of mid-1980s when unions were known to have fatally manhandle factory managers who failed to provide a cup of tea during the break.

While, in the longer term, some of the assets may have to be redefined, or reassessed to determine the continued value of such assets to the corporation, immediately they have to provide activity opportunities that can have a multiplier effect on building the turnaround tempo.

The choice of activity must therefore be strategic and not tactical, arising from a clear, unambiguous mission statement to ensure that all resources are directed towards the same goal to achieve meaningful results.

Rooted to the realities, the mission, at this stage, is unlikely to be awe-inspiring, but will still demand new ways of looking at the market and an innovative assessment of the company's strengths. The activity plan will necessarily venture into doing things differently from before, but will have to be based firmly within the ambit of the presently doable, rather than the most desirable.

MY FIRST SIX MONTHS AT HMV

When I drove into the sprawling grounds of Gramophone Co. of India Ltd. (HMV), in Dum Dum, a suburb of Kolkata, just beyond the airport, on a mid-November morning, I had quite a few trepidations.

The company driver who had fetched me from the hotel escorted me to my new office. Other than a few sombre faces who had looked at me with some curiosity when I was driven in, there was not a soul to be seen. It was nearing 9.30 a.m. and I had been told that the office starts at 9 a.m.

The office was a huge rectangle with a period desk at one end, a high backed throne at the far side and a few small visitor chairs. Anyone calling on the CEO would have to walk many yards, and if invited to sit, would be made to feel as if an audience has been granted. The breadth of the table required speaking at the top of one's voice but the general atmosphere was that of a funeral parlour, and I doubted whether anyone spoke above a whisper. Communication must have been a nightmare. Visitors were expected to come in through a musty anteroom that seated two secretaries, schooled no doubt in blocking visits. All in all, a baroque replica of a monarchy in decline.

As there was little of cheer, I decided to go walkabout. Fortunately, an apologetic VP, that of manufacturing, had by now arrived on the scene and reluctantly agreed to give me a tour of the premises. I could understand his reluctance as we moved from workshop to workshop, with little to see, other than clusters of idlers standing by machines in need of maintenance, and sporadic signs of activity with no particular aim in sight.

What, I asked, was the most pressing problem? No monies, I was told, to buy raw materials. If you had raw materials can you produce to capacity, I asked. Not really was the answer, as most of the machines needed servicing. Apparently, lack of spares prevented the routine servicing that sensitive electronic cassette duplicating machines required. But I said the machines are fairly new. They are, but then the workers did not know how to handle them, as the American supplier's installation and training team never made it to the factory, a matter of paying airfares and hotel bills. If that is sorted out, do you have enough orders? Not quite, as sales has stopped sending new orders to production as previous orders remained unexecuted.

By this time, we had reached a huge warehouse that turned out to be the finished goods store and it appeared stacked. How? Before the monies dried up, it was considered good practice to make economic batch sizes. Such batch sizes always exceeded orders, and the warehouse was full of excess production units. Are there no repeat orders? No reply.

There were a few other stores stacked to the ceilings with more cassettes, records, record sleeves and so on. One had shining metal records, something I had never seen before. These turned out to be the matrixes of the original sound tracks from which records are pressed and tapes are processed for making cassettes. Of value, I asked. Yes, was the answer, if the sales chaps get orders for old favourites, which happen once in a while.

The next couple of weeks were spent on more fact finding. The one consistent message was no money. The sales team had stopped visiting dealers, as their orders were not met. New albums were not being recorded as the artists refused to sing unless some back royalty payments were cleared. Machines were lying idle because of no raw materials.

What about the vast store of nostalgic music lying in the stores? Oh, they sell, I was told, but the demand is small and pirates, illegal copiers, were supplying these to the market at lower prices.

'Have I stumbled on to an under-utilized asset?' asked a tiny voice within me. If HMV can somehow protect its sole reproduction rights of these numbers, it may, just may, have a competitive edge.

I had to find a light at the end of the tunnel, and the path thereto. And I had very little time to get moving. Activity is what was needed to snap the company out of the state of shell shock, and that too an activity that reached out to all corners of the company, all the idle units and offices, executives and workers.

It had to be a simple rallying point—relevant, exciting if possible and certainly doable. The company, demoralized as it was with battered and bruised managers and insecure workers, was not ready to work towards a grand vision. The level of scepticism was high in direct contrast to its level of confidence, which was rock bottom.

FINDING A DOABLE TASK

The challenge for me was to create some confidence by embarking on an activity that would demonstrate to the company that it could live to do battle another day.

The selected activity had to focus on the fundamentals of the business—revenue generation and control of costs. It needed to be designed in a manner that would increase the involvement and productivity of the whole organization, or at the very least, a large number of the workforce.

The asset balance sheet that I could see at this point of time were the formidable archive of vintage music and an assortment of physical assets and process capabilities that could produce, in-house, all the components of recorded music, after a fashion.

The company had never fully exploited the market opportunity for its library of vintage music, as it continued to invest in creating new albums in its hay days. This turned up to be a high-risk strategy, as the company was unable to market the new albums profitably in significant volumes, owing to its inability to switch over from vinyl records to cassettes. As a result, such investments remained unrecovered.

Faced with a severe resource crunch, which precluded acquisition or production of new albums, we were forced into rebuilding the company on the strength of the archives, known in the trade as 'back catalogue'. Trade visits, especially among upmarket music dealers, which catered to the demands of the connoisseur, confirmed that there indeed was a niche for such products, even though the dealers were sceptical about the company's ability to package the catalogue products in a way that will be acceptable to the discerning buyer.

The sales team acknowledged that the back catalogue is saleable, but was quick to point out that volumes will be low, as the bulk of the trade wanted new sound tracks. The trade, they felt, perceived back catalogue as slow but steady sellers, presently made available by illegitimate and unauthorized copiers, 'pirates' cheaply. Pirates of course happily used the company records or cassettes as source material.

The marketing team, now strengthened by a mid-level manager brought in to underpin the incumbent VP, was convinced of the back catalogue potential but unsure of the appeal of back catalogue products sold in standard packaging at a price higher than pirates. Pirate prices incidentally were lower than even the component costs incurred by the company at that stage.

CATALOGUE AS AN ASSET

The scenario that emerged could be summarized as follows:

1. Discerning buyers buy back catalogue and pay a better price.
2. Back catalogue needs to be presented differently.
3. Competition is from pirates who do not have access to original sound tracks.

There seemed to be an opportunity to market a special pack aimed at a target audience that was bonded together with the desire for a uniform genre of music.

After some debate, the genres shortlisted were Indian classical music, Western classical music, old Hindi film soundtracks and Carnatic classical music, all of which our archives had in plenty. The consensus further moved towards developing a multi-cassette pack that could bear the cost of additional value addition—a gift pack and background literature on the evolution of the genre, that connoisseurs seemed to appreciate. Such a pack would be seen as a collector's item and would fetch, or so was the hope, a much higher unit price.

However, the genre that was finally selected to drive this 'new product concept' was 'Rabindra sangeet'—songs written and composed by Rabindranath Tagore, the only Indian literature Nobel Laureate.

The company had a tradition of releasing a number of new albums of Tagore's songs on his birth anniversary. As it so happened, the 125th birth anniversary of Tagore was coming up in a five months' time, and the release of a collection of old favourites was seen at least as a continuation of this tradition, the novelty of the concept perhaps making up for the company's inability to commission new albums.

TASK FORCES

Once the product focus was agreed, task forces were created to design the product—the compilation details, the pack options, research on background literature and so on. There was one overriding requirement—in-house facilities had to be used as no outside resources were available. A weekly progress meeting schedule was agreed as well, as the launch date, determined by the poet's birth anniversary, was imminent.

The newness of the project greatly helped break down territorial boundaries, and all the task forces were drawn from various disciplines. Marketing, A&R (Artists & Repertoire), sales and the studio interacted with each other for song selection and writing up the background material. Marketing, production, purchase and finance teamed up to look for packaging options and material sourcing. A human resources manager, the only other mid-level manager hired in this period to underpin an ineffective VP, volunteered to find ways of redeploying the workforce to do a variety of jobs in-house, to make the task achievable.

THE PROGRESS

The first weekly meeting had a mix of good news and bad.

The concept was taking shape as a tour de force of the genius of Tagore, bound to appeal to the connoisseur. However, a minimum of 12 cassettes was required to do justice to the theme. A 12-cassette pack would have a price tag well above what the dealers were prepared to stock, and the concern was that dealers might actually break the gift pack and sell individual cassettes thus destroying the collector's item theme. That apart the initial volume input to the trade would be small and repeat business would be adversely affected, as pirated copies would no doubt flood the market after our release.

The marketing department had designed excellent material for backup literature that would really come alive in multi-colour brochures. But the in-house print shop could at best print two colour jobs.

Production and marketing came up with a presentation box made out of wood and board, which looked very good, but would add significantly to the cost if the normal outer pack for a cassette, a plastic 'library box', was retained. We had to find a way to use the wooden box, not only because it looked good, but it also did two other things— use waste materials lying around in the carpentry shop, and provide work for the large number of dedicated carpentry shop workmen.

Human resources reported success in persuading the assembly plant workers to work on a retrieval programme, that would enable dismantling and reassembly of large quantities of unsold cassettes. These could then be used as cassette shells for the new products. The retrieval programme would provide work to some of the less skilled record plant workmen in addition to the workforce assigned to the assembly plant.

Engineering reported that it had started repairing some of the defective parts of the cassette duplication and moulding equipment in the engineering section and should get most of the machines in working order when the company was ready to roll.

We had come a long way in a week.

Consensus on a few contentious issues was reached relatively quickly, such as dispensing with the library box and packing individual cassettes in paperboard cartons. This made the wooden boxes affordable.

Marketing initially resisted the printing section manager's suggestion that all packaging items and product literature are printed in-house in two-tone sepia, using stocks of board and paper lying in the factory. But the fact that this would generate productive work for the idle printing shop workmen persuaded them to redesign the artworks.

A CHANGE IN DISTRIBUTION STRATEGY

We had not yet found a way around the distribution problem—dealer resistance to buy reasonable volumes at the high unit price that the collector's item would be priced at. Nor did we have an answer to the piracy problem that would crop up as soon as the first batches reached the market. Additionally, dealers would want credit and that would mean tying up working capital in a new format, a first in the market and therefore a risk.

That is, till such time someone suggested selling to the customer directly, bypassing the dealer. In fact, we can do one better, and announce a subscription scheme—a la magazines—pay now and get your special collector set later.

Tempting, but did we have the credibility left for customers to pay money upfront? The answer was no.

But we resolved that after a round of discussions with one of our bankers, who agreed to take the deposits and act as a delivery point when the packs would be ready.

We were now all set to go, with a goal, a game plan that gainfully utilized over 90 per cent of our workforce, and an enthusiasm that even our bankers shared.

THE RESULTS

Fortunately, this was a very successful activity. It was profitable, cash came in before production, the factory became a beehive of activity and large quantities of dead inventory were recycled. The company was back in business as customers showed their appreciation placing large orders.

The company also gained in other ways.

1. *The company learnt the true value of its assets—the archives, and in it, the company found a sustainable competitive advantage, the exploitation of which over the years has made it again the number one music company.*

2. *The activity provided the opportunity to bring about a structural and a cultural change in the organization by adopting a multi-discipline participative decision-making process, and sharing responsibilities and accountabilities.*

3. *The company learnt the value of speed in acting. A sick company cannot take too much time in pondering over proposed action; neither can it afford bureaucratic red tape delaying such action.*

4. *The basic discipline of organized thinking was reinforced. Procedures were simplified to facilitate quick decision-making. A one page, simple form which stated the problem, the proposed solution, the team responsible for action, the activity time frame and estimated costs helped people focus on the task and remain committed to completion on time and within budget. A follow up one-page report stating the results achieved, further strengthened the planning discipline and created a data bank for future reference.*

5. *The activity opened new horizons for reaching out to the customer. In the process, it galvanized the traditional music dealers to be more co-operative to the company, to protect their own future business interests.*

6. *The bankers and other stakeholders were persuaded that the company was able to work its way out of trouble, and co-operated both in making the activity a success and participating in future fund raising plans.*

7. *The Union showed its willingness to co-operate if the management showed positive intent to find a way forward.*

OTHER OPTIONS

Easier short-term options were available to the company. The back catalogue could be licensed to competitors for a royalty payment. This is a fairly standard practice in international markets, and the company had tried this in the past, with limited success. Not having a valuation method established, the company could only get token license fees.

Alternatively, the catalogue could be milked, packaged in standard cassettes and sold at heavily discounted prices to the trade as a counter to the pirate threat.

None of these alternatives would have resulted in a core activity to form a platform for future growth. Neither would these actions involve the total organization to participate in the reconstruction process.

The Second Priority

COST MANAGEMENT

Cost Management can never be the first priority of any turnaround manager. Focusing on cutting costs in general, when revenues are shrinking, only exacerbate the problems. Not knowing whether there is a way forward, concentrating on cutting costs can be totally counterproductive. It further demoralizes a company already saddled with a heavy cross-immediate closure, loss of jobs and livelihoods looming large.

HMV was fortunate in having a number of resources on hand— the archives to create a product, stocks of 'waste' material and unused inventory as raw material (accountants will violently disagree) and facilities to develop differentiations in packaging.

But some of these resources were also cash drains—the worker wage bill being one such. In a political climate where even temporary layoffs were subject to government permission, which weren't forthcoming, these were fixed costs, with no credit available. Paydays were sacrosanct, and caused more sleepless nights than any other deadlines.

However, achieving better gross margins can and should be an immediate priority.

While it was apparent that matching competitively benchmarked material costs, manufacturing, distribution and marketing efficiencies may take some time, urgent steps had to be taken in pruning other operating costs to generate the cash required for the renewal programme. Here was an opportunity to usher in some changes in the work ethics and the culture as well.

As in most other companies, a number of operating cost elements were not treated as strategic issues at HMV.

The buyer was satisfied working towards controlling input costs in line with historical trends, which in turn was in line with inflation. For him, reduction in input costs was an unfair strategic objective; he had not, for example, studied pirate prices, an obvious conclusion from which would have been that pirates are able to source their materials cheaply. And that there was an opportunity in enabling the company adopt a more aggressive pricing strategy, if the input costs could be brought down to pirate levels.

The production manager was equally unprepared to recognize an increase in per man productivity as a strategic objective. There was no competitive manning analysis available, and the norms had remained unchanged from time studies conducted some time earlier in association with a national productivity council expert. As far as the production manager was concerned these norms were non-negotiable, and he had set a trend of paying overtime and employing casuals whenever any pressure built up on production. Typically, such practices resulted in regular overtime payments, and salaries for casuals even when, as now, the work pressure was low.

Across the board, no manager was willing to take responsibility for reducing travel, utility or communication costs. These were perceived as non-strategic annual budget items, already pared to the bone and further deliberation on this issue was seen as a waste of time.

I had to find a way to raise pruning of operating costs to a strategic level. These expenses needed to be linked to results. They needed to be taken out of 'overheads'—the no man's land—and reallocated as a prime cost element and therefore a responsibility of the functional manager. This required reworking the costing methods and it was obvious that bottom-up support was necessary to make the new costing formula acceptable.

The focus was on first defining the operating costs that are within the control of the employees; that is to separate the costs of running the business from those expense heads where the company personnel cannot make any immediate or meaningful contribution, such as interest burdens and depreciation. These are the wages of past management sin. The employees can do very little to alter these. I had to take the onus of tackling these issues separately.

A company wise wake-up call was necessary in creating a competitive cost consciousness. A pay cut across the board would have been an

*ideal wake-up call. Based in Kolkata, with a very pro-labour govern-
ment and strong labour unions, this was not possible.*

*But an executive salary and perquisites cut or deferment was pos-
sible, and these were implemented. The executive lunch rooms were
closed; company cars withdrawn and salary payments were deferred
whenever the need arose.*

*The leave entitlements were redefined. Labour laws not only spec-
ified a minimum number of days as privilege leave, but also made it
mandatory to allow a certain number of days as casual leave, and a
further number of days as medical leave, all with pay. Earlier managements had at some stage introduced the concept of encashment of
unavailed leave days, including casual and medical leave days.*

*Once again the unionized workers were protected, but some changes
were possible. Casual leave and medical leave for executives were abol-
ished, but departmental managers were empowered to give days off,
with pay, if persuaded that there was a genuine need. Further accumu-
lation of privilege leave was stopped, and executives were encouraged
to use up leave due to them, especially accumulated leave. Eventually it
resulted in some salary savings.*

*Overtime sanctions were stopped and casual employees were asked
to go.*

*In the context of the problems facing the company, these were at best
cosmetic changes as real cost savings were not large. But these moves
set the tone for a change in the mindset of the company.*

*The real cost management started once the company's efficiencies
were benchmarked against competition. Cross-functional task forces
drawn from the company's management pool, supported and super-
vised by outside consultants, were sent to study work norms at supplier's and even competitors, including the pirate-in-chief's factories. This
became a continuous practice, and union representation in these task
forces, eventually became possible, though in the early days the union
resisted any such move. The focus was to understand and emulate the
work practices of the best-managed companies in the business.*

*Such benchmarking requires fairly detailed studies of every aspect
of the operation, and is time consuming, and has to be a continuous
process. Dissemination of interim findings and implementation of operational changes therefore became necessary.*

I found a Monday morning stand-up half hour meeting, requiring the presence of at least one executive from each department discussing cost containment very effective.

The task forces presented their topline findings and immediately implementable suggestions. The other attendees were asked to commit to implementation for their operations there and then, with specific targets for the week.

The momentum picked up in a few weeks, when actual cost reductions achieved in the previous weeks were reported and the concerned executives duly applauded. This set the ball rolling for more suggestions and recommendations, ready acceptance of the following weeks' targets and an environment of healthy competition among the different departments to come up with further plans.

These meetings also highlighted specific lack of skills and training needs for both executives and workers were identified. Training became a regular part of the rehabilitation programme.

Soon, a hitherto taboo issue, excess manpower cost, became a recurring theme at such meetings. The need for rightsizing for survival became apparent to all. Eventually, when the conditions were conducive to implement a rightsizing scheme, I had the support of the entire organization.

The Third Priority

FUNDING THE RENEWAL

The CEO has to make the company understand that immediate activity generation and cost reductions are not an end in itself.

The real objective is to create the ability to increase revenues and gain market share. This takes time, and investment in marketing and product development. Efficient cost management will free the resources required to market the company's products better. Unless the company understands why revenue increases will take some more time, not only would the cost containment effort be half-hearted, but the marketing and sales team will become the butt of cruel jokes, and no sick company has ever recovered with a demoralized sales and marketing team.

Improving liquidity is therefore a precondition to any rehabilitation project.

*Cash in the business is like the biblical talent; it is death to hide,
especially in a sick company. The balance sheet is a good place to
look for such 'hidden talents' as it often is the graveyard for burying
under-utilized assets.*

I was fortunate to have Anand Dhawan as a financial consultant.

*Anand was different from the typical financial consultant. He
preferred smart casuals to pinstripe suits. He carried his disdain for
conventional wisdom on his monogrammed sleeves, and spoke in a
monotonous, often infuriating drone.*

*To him, every cost item was a revenue opportunity. Every dollar
spent in running of the business must earn two dollars in revenue. If
that is not happening across the board Anand was worried.*

*A downtown office, owned or leased, is a cash opportunity. Anand
had us move out of our downtown sales office in Bombay to the suburbs,
and generated incremental cash by subleasing the downtown office, that
too with nine years' rent paid in advance!*

*For Anand, equipment is tied up cash, and depreciation benefits are
of little immediate concern to a sick and loss making company. Anand
would have loved to persuade a leasing company to buy some of our
machines and lease them back to the company for use. Unfortunately,
a sick company often has its physical assets hypothecated to the banks,
as was the case in our company. But other turnaround managers should
bear this in mind. Upfront cash for productive utilization will generate
many times more cash than the lease rentals the company would pay
on leasing back their 'own' equipment.*

*However, Anand saw an under-utilized intangible asset, in some
of our repertoire library, which we could not exploit in the short term,
and arranged the 'sale' of these for cash up front and a 'lease back in
perpetuity' for our use.*

*Anand fumed at doubtful debts and put a recovery team in place.
To him, writing-off even half to get the balance half as cash in hand is a
good bargain. 'Remember each dollar spent effectively would generate
two dollars. The written-off half would be earned back in no time' was
his mantra. Anand had no patience with debtors matching industry
norms. He insisted on immediate realization offering a substantial cash*

discount. *After all the dollars lost will be recovered by the extra dollars freed to do business with!*

Anand would have loved to charge a hefty fee as a retainer. But I had learnt my lesson from the master, and agreed to pay only a success fee and no retainer up front!

THE BIGGEST LESSON

The biggest lesson we learnt was that disruptions will happen. Remember this was long before the term was coined and bandied about.

Some can be anticipated. Music cassettes appeared in international markets long before it reached the Indian market. HMV may have been able to play a role in persuading the government not to reserve pre-recorded cassettes for small scale industries, and thus keep piracy within limits. A lot of my time was spent on fighting piracy, organizing raids by a recalcitrant police force and fighting court cases in front of judges, one of whom actually said in his order, that the pirate is doing a social service by making music available at affordable prices!

The second big lesson we learnt was that we were a music company, and not a record or cassette company.

By late 1980s, digitization of music had begun. Compact discs (CDs) had made an appearance. It was only a matter of time for the technology to make discs that will be freely and cheaply available.

We did two things right. One was to surrender a license I had inherited, to manufacture magnetic tapes in-house. There was no way we were going to build a plant to produce something which may soon become obsolete.

The second was to invest in digitizing our music catalogue instead of setting up a CD processing plant. This is paying off in spades even now, as royalties earned from song downloads on devices have become the primary revenue source for all music companies.

A Recap

A quick recap of turnaround fundamentals may be worth repeating first.

A turnaround manager's primary task is to transform a demoralized organization into a fighting unit ready to revitalize the company.

Cash is critical. It needs to be preserved for initiating only revenue-generating activities. Settling past dues cannot be given priority.

If fresh fund inflow is inadequate, resources have to mobilize from within; a careful audit of assets and innovative utilization of such assets is often the only option.

The renewal process begins with sharp focus on an immediate positive, revenue multiplying, activity involving as many people as possible.

The company can move beyond a turnaround phase only when a sustainable business model is ready for implementation.

CHAPTER 3

A TALE OF PASSION
THE BHARAT TILES STORY

Sajid Peerbhoy, a good friend of mine, called me out of the blue one evening to say that he has suggested to Mrs Dilnavaz Variava, owner/chairperson of a cement floorings and tiles company, based in Mumbai, that she calls me as I am a 'turnaround specialist'. Sajid then went on to describe Bharat Floorings and Tiles' (BFT) operation and shared the top and bottom line numbers of the company which left me rather intrigued. Can I put my arms around such a 'boutique' operation and add value and will BFT be able to afford my very modest fees!

It may be an opportunity to check out whether the principles of turnaround management, as I understood them, apply to even small companies with far less complexities? I was inclined to put it to a test, as long as it did not impinge too much on my schedule.

By the time Mrs Variava called me the next evening, BFT's product range displayed on their website had impressed me enough to believe that both their top and bottom lines should rightfully be many times more than what they were, and I could help make that happen. By the time the call ended, the other question was also answered. No, even my scaled down fees would wipe out their profits. But we agreed to work together subject to Firdaus, her son, and co-owner's nod, and by deferring my fees to when the company could afford it!

BFT was born out of passion at a time when India, then the Jewel in the Crown of the British Empire, was waking up to the call for independence, political as well as economic.

Swadeshi, home-made, was the mantra propagated by Mahatma Gandhi, who urged young Indians to 'make in India' and get out of the economically disastrous cycle of exporting raw materials cheap and importing finished goods with exorbitant markups.

One starry eyed young man, Pherozeshah Sidhwa, with inspiration and help from Jamshed Nusserwanjee Mehta, a colleague of Mahatma Gandhi, decided to chuck his articleship as a lawyer and set up a cement tile production unit. His nephew, Rustom, equally bullish about Swadeshi, did not ponder too long before joining his uncle's venture. Naming the unit was a no-brainer. It had to be Bharat Floorings and Tiles, with the map of the then undivided India stamped on the back of every tile, for emphasis.

As it so happened, the Sidhwa family owned large sheds in a tiny hamlet called Uran, to distil liquor from *mogra* (jasmine) and rose flowers, oranges and other fruits, in the traditional way, a technology dictated by the absence of electricity and running water. These sheds suddenly became available as the Raj (the British government), in yet another attempt to stifle local production, imposed prohibition and banned the production of any liquor.

Early Days

The year was 1922.

Pherozeshah and Rustom set up their tile-making shop in one of these unused sheds. The fact that the only links with Bombay (now Mumbai), the nearest market for the tiles, were fair weather fishing boats, caused little anguish to these two young entrepreneurs who immediately set about peddling their wares to the dignitaries of Bombay many of whom happened to be brother Parsees. As far as the technology was concerned, the tiles were handcrafted and then hydraulically pressed on machines run with electricity from diesel generators installed by them. The Sidhwas modestly aimed to be 'equal to the world's best', a standard high enough for the company to swear not to ever compromise on quality, and attractive enough for would be customers to cancel their import orders.

Pherozeshah's commitment to his quality norms was severely tested soon after starting, when he chose to stop the dispatch of a batch of black and white tiles made for Sir Cowasji Jehangir's New Readymoney Mansion (Flora Fountain/Hutatma Chowk), Mumbai. He then ensured that everyone around got the message when he took a dramatic step—the entire batch was thrown into the sea.

The factory was closed while he visited Italy with a sample tile only to find that the problem did not lie with the discarded tiles but with their polishing!

The tiles from the new batch, polished more carefully this time around, still shine in a few parts of the building, a good 90 odd years after they were made in the Uran factory! BFT also learnt to lay and polish their own tiles to avoid a repeat of this experience.

As the years rolled by, BFT continued to tile many princely residences and palaces for the Maharajas of Bansda, Bikaner, Gwalior, Jodhpur, Kolhapur, to name a few. Even the British could not resist using BFT's 'swadeshi' tiles in their governors' houses, universities, the Mint and other public buildings.

The next decade, 1930–40, may well have been called the renaissance decade. As Hollywood entered the country with a bang, Bombay saw a number of new cinema houses—Metro, Eros, Regal, Excelsior, Broadway, Capitol and Roxy—all tiled by BFT.

Those years saw the birth of the art deco phase of architecture for which Mumbai has global recognition. Almost every building in the art deco precincts of Oval, Marine Drive, Malabar Hill, Altamount Road and other places across Mumbai and beyond had BFT tiles. BFT however remained a handcrafted tile-making company and volumes remained small.

As World War II gathered momentum, the government diverted cement to defence installations. BFT tiles, deprived of their basic raw material, had to almost close down.

Showing a remarkable nimbleness of feet, Pherozeshah and Rustom, lacking cement to make tiles, struck a deal with two stranded Czechs, who used to supply them grinding wheels, to start India's first grinding wheel company, (Grindwell Abrasives now Grindwell Norton Ltd) operating from the Uran factory of BFT tiles.

Post War Years

After the war, when cement was once again available, BFT restarted its tile manufacture. The Uran factory was bursting at the seams, with tiles coming from one end and grinding wheels from the other.

BFT needed its own space, and moved to Bombay, and remained there for many years, producing tiles for the burgeoning city and a newly independent India. Its mosaic/terrazzo tiles were in iconic buildings from the seat of government to prestigious homes.

A factory was set up in Kurla in 1955 to make cement tiles and another unit was set up in Sewri for marble processing. 'Bharat Tiles & Marble' regained its position as a premier supplier of quality cement and marble floors.

The 1970s saw the skyline of Bombay changing rapidly as villas and bungalows, the owners of which were BFT's core customers, made way for high rise office and residential buildings, with builders looking for new technologies which allowed them to build faster and finish quicker.

Cement tiles have a minimum thirty-five-day cycle from manufacture to laying and polishing the surface. Ceramic and vitrified tiles, new entrants in the market since the late 1960s, were available off the shelf and could be laid in 24 hours. Builders naturally opted for ceramic tiles for low end and natural marble for high end apartments in these new buildings. Bharat was under pressure and responded by shifting focus to making factory floorings and chequered tiles for outdoor use. Unfortunately, this high volume, low margin product range was vulnerable to cheaper cottage sector competitors, and BFT's continuance came under threat.

By the mid-1990s, the Sidhwa/Variava families had to take a call on what to do with their various businesses. The tiles business was making losses and the company was sustained primarily by an ancillary warehousing business. The majority of shareholders wished to close down the tiles business and sell off the properties along with the warehousing business. That is when Dilnavaz decided to acquire total control of the tile business and a small cement tile unit was set up in Thane district near Mumbai, for manufacturing of tiles by a couple of loyal former employees, more out of passion than for profits, which were hard to come by.

Heritage™ Makes a Comeback

Serendipity, a word rarely found in management books, helped Dilnavaz find a market niche which enabled her to bring new life to the tiles business.

BFT tiles are handcrafted with a minimal use of simple machines, primarily a ball mill to mix Portland grey and white cement, stone chips and dyes and hydraulic presses to press a top designed layer on a hardy grey cement base. What sets BFT's tiles apart are their designs, the precision with which stencils for the designs are made and the skill of the pressmen to fill the stencils and press them into exotic cement tiles which through a carefully controlled curing process become strong to withstand many footfalls over the years, often longer than 50 years.

While some of the 'scrap' moved from Uran to Sewri and Kurla, little attention was paid to stacks of stencils not used since the company moved out of Uran and changed its business model to focus on art deco, then mosaic and high volume chequered and sturdy outdoor tiles. Going through the factory storage areas, when the shareholders were contemplating closure of the business, Dilnavaz saw some beautiful old brass stencils of the designs first introduced to India by BFT in the 1920s which were forgotten but in good shape and ready to be used.

Dilnavaz seized the opportunity to relaunch the colourfully designed tiles as BFT's Heritage™ range for discerning customers, as a different offering from the mass market flooring solutions. The colour palette was expanded to suit contemporary tastes. These helped the company to inch towards breaking even.

Firdaus had also joined the business and brought with him much needed design flair, as well as enough IT savvy to build a website which succeeded in bringing out the design excellence of BFT tiles.

But for some strange reason, more than a decade after the introduction of its Heritage™ tiles, BFT seemed to be stuck in the groove of making low end heavy duty cement tiles and mosaic tiles, vainly trying to compete with ceramic tiles against seemingly insurmountable price and delivery schedule odds.

That was when Dilnavaz, Firdaus and I got together and sat down to the mundane routine of turning this company around to become a profitable venture.

The Turnaround Strategy

Almost all turnarounds require an asset utilization strategy. Simply because a turnaround candidate is always short of funds to invest in any of the critical needs to embark on a growth trajectory.

The critical needs may vary from company to company, but will centre around acquiring new technology, upgrading design and research capability, capacity building often requiring additional equipment, revamping the organization by rightsizing, again at a cost, retraining the existing workforce, hiring new talent and promoting the products and services on offer.

An asset utilization strategy is the only means available to an under-performing company to generate the cash flow in the short term to tackle any of the above-mentioned needs.

The first task at BFT therefore was to audit our assets.

This did not take too long. In terms of tangible assets, BFT was and still is a very asset-light company. The office and the plants are in rented premises. Given the manufacturing process, the plant and machinery required only a small investment already depreciated to a virtually nil value. The manufacturing was contracted to experienced past employees.

However, there was some discussion on the intangible assets. There may or may not have been brand value, but in a turnaround this is a limited asset.

The next task was to get a fix on BFT's positioning in the market and see whether this can be leveraged to sustain a turnaround attempt.

The building industry in India was booming. The market for floorings was conservatively estimated to be anywhere between two and five billion dollars. But BFT did not really need to know the size of this market. By definition, given the nature of its manufacturing process, BFT was destined to be a niche player. The question was which niche?

The bulk of the market comprised natural stones—marble, granite and kota and factory made ceramic or vitrified tiles—both Indian and cheap Chinese imports. Cement tiles were on the way out from the indoor floor tiles segment, but hung in there as paving stones and other outdoor applications.

There were a few other indoor cement tile manufacturers, small units based in Gujrat and Rajasthan, servicing nearby markets given the exorbitant transportation costs owing to the weight of each cement tile. The combined volumes of all these units, including BFT, were too small to claim to be a segment by itself.

So how and where does BFT position itself? Can it create a niche, albeit tiny, for itself? What would the building blocks be?

BFT's strengths were not many. The technology was unchanged over the years and not amenable to easy scaling up. Artificial floorings namely ceramic and others were produced in bulk, sold at prices possible for large volume players, easy to lay, cheap too, to the end consumer as these did not require polishing after laying, as marble or cement floors do, and a boon for builders who did not have to wait for six weeks for a floor to be finished before handing over to the buyers.

Designer tiles appeared to be a possible niche to explore. But there were some traditional designer tiles which sold at ridiculously low prices, thus putting such tiles in a 'cheap' category. BFT needed to create a premium designer tiles category for itself. BFT's Heritage™ tiles could provide the leverage we were looking for.

The Heritage™ tiles had two distinct advantages to provide BFT the building blocks to launch a turnaround initiative: first, designs, moulds and stencils which made the tiles a success when they were first launched. BFT had quite a few of those ranging from two, three or four colour designs, and second, the technology which provided BFT the easy flexibility to change the colour combinations to suit customer preferences thus offering a 'customized' tile to the end user a possibility.

That apart, the fact that these tiles were handcrafted and provided a livelihood to artisans had an emotional appeal to a section of the target user audience. If only an exotic story can be built around these two pluses and reach out to potential customers who were willing to pay a premium over the factory produced, mass market, vitrified and ceramic tiles, there was a possible window of opportunity. And as it happens with premium products, in time the premium alone becomes a draw, providing the user a unique kind of satisfaction.

The rather lukewarm response to the earlier relaunch of the Heritage™ range of tiles was perhaps due to BFT's dependence on old customers for new orders. Unfortunately, many of the architects and interior designers of old had retired by the time the Heritage™ tiles made their way back to the market. A few, still in business, had assumed that BFT ceased to exist.

The new generation of architects engaged in designing custom-made homes needed to be reintroduced to BFT's tiles, and persuaded that the exotic new range of tiles could actually raise a rather plain apartment to another level—a dream home bringing in a touch of exotica from the Mediterranean seafront villas such as Spain and Morocco, Granada and Genoa, fit for 'kings and queens' even when used in tandem with the mass produced monochrome ceramic tiles. And that, such tiles will necessarily come at a premium price.

The order flow for BFT followed a set pattern. Architects designed villas for private owners or condominiums for builders and housing societies, where individuals bought apartments and often wanted to remodel these. The architect was therefore the prime mover in generating business for BFT. Of course, the end buyer had the final say, and a few of them actually took the flooring decision by themselves, persuading the architect, if one was involved, to include BFT in their specs.

Having evolved a possible repositioning the question was whether the present organization had the capability to reach out to the large numbers of architects operating out of the major cities.

An audit of the organization, its processes and its people became the next focus.

Like all small companies, BFT was very light in management bandwidth.

Dilnavaz, the owner chairman, had a number of other interests and did not have the time to focus on the business and had therefore delegated the day-to-day running of the business to a few trusted aides.

Faiyaz Mukhtiar, a chartered accountant by training, was the GM ops, overseeing manufacture, procurement, sales support, administration, finance and company secretarial work. A lot of his time was also spent in supervising the approved contractors' installation work. He barely had time to breathe let alone strategize for the future. Faiyaz was also under pressure to make sure that the company at least broke even to avoid the embarrassment of going to the chairman, hand-in-hand, to ask for bail outs. As a result, he was totally risk averse. Firdaus was the head of marketing, full of ideas for new products and comfortable with the digitized world, having introduced a number of innovations in making sales presentations and creating a brilliant interactive website. He also had built up excellent rapport with the new generation of architects and was responsible for getting the bulk of business for the high-end tiles and new products.

The bigger problem was that it was not at all a process-driven company.

The company had a sales force comprising a general sales manager, sales reps in Mumbai city, Goa and Bangalore, calling on potential customers at random without a plan in place and no monitoring process to check either the GSM or the reps' day-to-day work schedules. The sales force was content chasing low hanging fruits by way of orders for wafer thin margin non-slip tiles from bulk buyers such as railways and municipal corporations. Most of these orders came towards the end of a financial year, and the factories, partially idle for quite a few months would have to go into overdrive, paying exorbitant overtime wages, to deliver on time. Wiping out the thin margins in the bargain!

Process implementation at various levels was the obvious priority. Getting competent people on board to share the workload of the very stretched management team was an equal priority. But these cost money, and take time.

BFT had neither. Not unusual for an under-performing company. Whatever BFT did, it had to be funded by internal accrual.

The first step had to be setting up a system which ensures a steady flow of orders.

In this business, getting an order was a time-consuming exercise. If an architect was sold on BFT's products, he or she would then include these in the designs submitted to the client. Should the client share the architect's enthusiasm for BFT's tiles, an enquiry would be generated along with a floor plan. This alone can take anywhere between one and six months.

A quotation along with detailed sketches of the floor plan would follow. Changes in drawings, price and delivery date negotiations may then take another one to three months. Then the order is generated.

It doesn't need a genius to figure out that the more balloons BFT has up in the air, that is, the more quotations it submits, the greater the chances of establishing a steady flow of orders.

Action? Go and get more enquiries. How? Meet more architects. How often? At least once a month, to keep BFT top of mind but not in your face all the time.

To begin with, BFT needed to define the universe of architects in Mumbai city, its biggest market.

The company records had names and addresses of barely 200 Bombay-based architects. A google search revealed many sources listing more than 1,500 Bombay-based architects, with names, addresses, telephone numbers and website URLs. Some of these contact details had to be verified, and took a fair amount of time to prepare a reliable roster of architects which was then divided into categories: Category A: high immediate potential; Category B: strong future potential and Category C: largely startups with some business potential.

The limited number of reps on the rolls determined the size of the universe which can be called upon with the desired frequency—1,000 architects. A rep could make eight calls in a working day, that is, 50 per week or 200 in a 4-week cycle, assuming each architect is contacted once in a journey cycle. In other words, each architect will receive 13 calls from a company rep in 52 weeks, enough to keep BFT top of mind, when designing projects.

The next task was to draw up daily architect visit schedules for the sales reps with 10 calls a day spread over A, B and C category in easily commutable geographic proximities.

The bigger task was to persuade the GSM and his team to buy into this plan. Neither was ready to accept the sudden imposition of order demanding accountability and forego a loose cannon approach to do business. Soon BFT was confronted with unannounced absenteeism, followed by resignations.

By then, Firdaus had identified a net-based sales force monitoring and management system and the company signed up for this system. Hiring new reps, willing to work in a process-driven manner, proved to be easy.

Eventually, when the GSM also wanted out, the top management got worried. But to their credit, they were willing to ride with the new system, especially as the new system cost less than half the GSM's annual salary, and the GSM was let go.

Responses to the new system in the early days were slow, partly because of the nature of the business, the time lag between detailing and generation of enquiries, and partly because a virtually new sales force took time to understand the nuances of the business and respond to non-standard enquiries, always a challenge when customers are promised customized tiles.

Having got the direct approach to architects in place, it was now time to put some pressure on the architect from the customer. Web enquiries, though small in numbers, suggested that for small projects, say reflooring one bedroom, end users often proceeded without the engagement of an architect or an interior decorator. Some of course wanted more details to be able to have a meaningful dialogue with their architects about more options. The most interesting finding was that such customers were not comparing prices of BFT's products with ceramic and other mass market flooring options. Their price point references were natural stones, that is, marble and granite, both selling at roughly twice the price of our Heritage™ tiles.

BFT was then persuaded to extend its reach to the end user by launching a small print campaign in specialized home décor magazines. The ads focused on the visual appeal of the Heritage™ floors set in an elitist ambience, with minimal copy. The content as well as the medium strongly emphasized the desired positioning, that of premium tiles. The campaign had an added bonus. Architects also saw these ads and concluded, without the company's prompting, that BFT tiles were indeed premium tiles, especially for those who had discerning tastes and budgets, and ignored small price increases that the company began making to be able to generate much needed funds to aggressively develop new designs for tiles and new products, such as cast-in-situ terrazzo floors.

Not unexpectedly, the biggest resistance to increase prices came from within, as the management had little confidence in their own products, and continued to neutralize the benefit of price increases by offering discounts, a malaise picked up during the company's days of selling cheap non-slip tiles. Unfortunately, indiscriminate discounting continues to this day.

The increased prices helped bolster BFT's premium image perception, and the higher margins helped giving salary hikes to the staff, a much needed morale booster and to raise the compensation of the senior managers to a level comparable to the market. More importantly, the company started generating enough cash to spend monies on further design and product development, and be able to participate in high-profile promotional events.

BFT is now engaged with an outstanding design house to continue the momentum through a rebranding exercise, and help BFT pleasantly surprise their clients with new designs and product concepts virtually every quarter.

BFT has come a long way since the three of us—Dilnavaz, Firdaus and I—got together to talk turnaround.

It is now a national brand extending its reach to all the major cities in the country.

A lot remains to be done and work goes on. BFT is now committed to progressing through process orientation, and has signed up for ISO certification to ensure quality adherence in all its functions prior to embarking upon an ambitious capacity building programme, which includes setting up production units in other parts of the country, and perhaps one in South East Asia.

By the way, BFT will end this fiscal with net profits, many, many times more than when Dilnavaz and I first talked on the phone.

CHAPTER 4

EARLY DISTRESS SIGNALS

CONSEQUENCES OF TURNING A BLIND EYE

'*Address books, video cameras, pagers, wristwatches, maps, books, travel games, flashlights, home telephones, dictation recorders, cash registers, Walkman, daytimers, alarm clocks, answering machines, yellow pages, wallets, keys, phrase books, transistor radios, personal digital assistants, dashboard navigation systems, remote controls, airline ticket counters, newspapers and magazines, directory assistance, travel and insurance agents, restaurant guides and pocket calculators.*

What do these things have in common?'

Ask Larry Downes and Paul Nunes, co-authors of *Big Bang Disruption*[1], and go on to point out that,

'*Each has, or is in the process of becoming, a victim of Big Bang Disruption, a new kind of innovation with the power to undermine stable businesses in a matter of months or even days'.*

Over time, many economists and business gurus have anticipated major disruptions caused by technology leaps, but would it be correct to accept that the rapidity with which technology

---

[1] Downes, Larry and Paul Nunes. 2014. Big Bang Disruption. Portfolio/Penguin.

innovations occur can and will undermine stable businesses in a matter of months or even days?

All business entities focus on satisfying market segments, that is, specific needs of a cross section of customers, which may begin small but in time grow big. The decision to address the needs of any particular market segment is almost always determined by the core assets and the core capabilities of the entrepreneur, the early birds reaping first mover advantages for a while. In time, the segment becomes large enough to become an industry, as a number of me-toos and other entrepreneurs enter these industries offering better products and services at lower prices.

Inevitably, the second and the third and the nth entrepreneur entering this segment bring in dramatic changes in the product introduced by the first mover and the method of doing business—primary success factors being manufacturing and distribution processes—to cater to the evolving needs of the market.

The industry is therefore always on the boil, resulting in a constant though mostly gradual transformation. All stable businesses, with capable managers, keep an eye on the changes and continuously tweak their business models to stay competitive. Sudden discontinuities can in fact be anticipated long before they become 'discontinuities'.

After years of research and conversations with senior managers in companies as diverse as Apple, IBM and De Beers among others, Professor Anita M. McGahan from Boston University concludes in her article 'How Industries Change',[2] that industries evolve along four distinct trajectories—radical, progressive, creative and intermediating. During the continuing evolution of an industry, threats are bound to emerge to a company's core activities (the recurring actions a company performs to attract and retain buyers and suppliers) and/or to its core assets (the durable assets which enable the company to efficiently perform the core activities), which shape the type of change the company will have to face.

---

[2] McGahan, Anita M. 2004. 'How Industries Change', Harvard Business Review, 82(10).

Radical changes occur, says Professor McGahan, when a company's core assets and core activities are both threatened with obsolescence.

A good example is that of a travel agency. Ability to book online tickets for planes and trains directly from the companies and emergence of web-enabled systems to book hotels, car hires and valet services offered by MakeMyTrip, Expedia, Travelocity and IRCTC have virtually eliminated smaller players from this industry. Big travel agencies such as Thomas Cook and Mercury Travels had to reinvent themselves as package tour operators to cater primarily to leisure travellers as opposed to business travellers, their erstwhile bread and butter customers. Thomas Cook in fact now operates an airline and cruise ships!

Progressive changes are forced upon companies when basic assets and activities remain stable, but new competitors bring in new levels of efficiency and offer products and services at such aggressive price points that many older companies have little option but to close down or sell out. Remember East-West Airlines, Damania Airways, ModiLuft, Air Deccan, Kingfisher Airlines at home and Pan Am, US Airways, Trans World Airlines (TWA) and others abroad? What happened to them were subversive attacks by new airlines offering on-time performances and services tailored to the needs of the basic traveller, with extras such as meals during flights, free check-in baggage allowances and other fringe benefits converted to 'paid' services. JetBlue, Southwest, IndiGo, Ryan and Jet are the new kids on the block disrupting the comfort world of many an airline which did not read the writing on the wall about the new flier profile and ignored the pressures to change.

Intermediating changes are those which affect primarily intermediaries. Online retailing is a good example of what it can do to well-established supermarkets chains and of course the hapless mom-and-pop shop owner.

Creative changes are those which disrupt industries almost overnight, to wit what smartphones have done to a number of industries. Even then, smartphones took 15 years to evolve from the early chunky mobile phones with 2-hour battery lives! Another example is the laptop, which began to nudge the PCs of table tops, and the mini version called tablets epitomized by the I-Pad, which certainly are pushing PCs to an early grave.

Conventional wisdom has no quarrel with Professor McGahan's concept of change and the trajectories thereof, having accepted the time-honoured premise that businesses have life cycles, and will inevitably fail someday. As if to lend credibility to such wisdom, businesses do fail, that too with monotonous regularity.

But the unpleasant fact for these soothsayers is that all businesses need not fail. In fact, some corporations have been around for a couple of centuries and longer. And post-mortems of those corporations who have been forced to shut down mostly point to inept management as the cause leading to closures. Ergo, businesses do not fail; people running these businesses fail.

When CEOs make a case to the stakeholders that the companies' performance has gone from poor to dismal because of cataclysmic changes in the industry, they are actually trying to cover up their own inability to take cognizance of the change agents in action, and the corporation's collective desire to bury their heads in sand.

There are however many exceptions especially in countries like India where the interference from the government and lack of clarity of some laws, especially those where more than one ministry is involved, create situations beyond the promoters' and the managers' control.

Recently, the Supreme Court of India demanded from the Reserve Bank of India (RBI) a list of defaulter companies, where the outstanding unserviced loans exceeded ₹500 crores (US$ 65 million at 2016 conversion rates).

RBI reluctantly provided such a list but with some cautionary riders: Most of the defaults are on infrastructure project loans.

1. Default has happened due to:

  1.1. delayed permission from government and regulatory agencies;

  1.2. delayed acquisition of land, again due to prevarications on land acquisition laws;

1.3. *delayed sanction of loans which made the borrower unable to use it in time (sic);*

1.4. *poor credit appraisal;*

1.5. *poor monitoring;*

1.6. *lack of business management knowledge;*

1.7. *unanticipated business cycle downturn;*

1.8. *commodity cycle downturn and*

1.9. *poor project execution.*

Source: Times of India news report on 30 March 2016

Point to note from the above-mentioned list is that barring 'lack of business management knowledge' and 'poor project execution' in all other cases, extraneous factors and the lending banks are responsible for creating a situation which led to the borrower default on repayments.

I would however hold the borrower responsible for citing 'unanticipated business cycle downturn' as a probable cause for justifying defaults.

In large corporations, such myopia leading to 'inability to take cognizance of the change agents in action, and the corporation's collective desire to bury their heads in sand' stems from a number of factors, some of which are worth revisiting before charting out a turnaround path.

Businesses Run Managers

It doesn't sound right, does it? Surely managers run businesses. That's why they are there.

Irrespective of who the stakeholders are, the decision-makers in a company are a small group of managers occupying key offices on the top floor, where the executive directors and CEOs and chief operating officers (COOs) operate from. Though all decisions are supposed to be cleared by a conclave of such managers through management committees and duly rubber stamped at board meetings, in practice a strong CEO, either the original promoter or a son/daughter of the promoter, retaining the backing of the largest shareholding block, becomes the modern day tsar, making all the decisions.

History tells us that typically the organization chart in such corporations resembles an amalgam of independent command modules. Communication follows rigid direct line reporting paths with interdepartmental interaction possible only at the top. As a result, the higher you go in the organization, the more insulated you are from the customer and the front-line people who interact with them. And CEOs are often so isolated that they remind you of poker players raising antes blind.

Unfortunately, any hierarchical organization, be it the government, the church, a political party or a business corporation, fosters an environment where communication channels are jealously guarded. Thus, the old saying, 'knowledge is power' gains a new sinister interpretation.

Consequently, the CEO is rarely allowed to interact directly with any level below the general manager. Similarly, the general managers are also restricted to direct interaction with one, or at best two, levels below them. In social cultures, such as those prevailing in Asian countries, if the CEO insists on meeting executives down the line, he is required to invite the line bosses as well. Effectively, such meetings end up being another forum where only the boss's views are aired and defended.

The extent of isolation becomes more pronounced as the hierarchy fans out further within each department. Even a medium-sized organization with a couple of factories and a few regional offices would have complex structures, marketing, manufacturing and finance, HR, logistics, all reporting to respective VP/directors, each very protective of their own little empires.

The early proponents of such hierarchical structures such as armies realized very quickly that 'communication channel protocols', must be established to ensure, if nothing else, that no deviation from the basic rule 'an order must be followed to the letter' is ever permitted.

In traditional corporations, these communication channel protocols are thick-bound volumes, the manuals which spell out in excruciating detail the high command's dictat on every-thing a line manager can and cannot do, ranging from requisi-tioning a pencil to suspending an employee for dereliction of duty.

These manuals do not tell the employee how to win and retain customers, but explain at great length how form G114 needs to be filled and approved by the immediate boss, and his/her boss before going on a business trip and how form G115, the expense statement, must be submitted within 48 hours of return from said business trip with three photocopies of all vouchers. There's no urgency to file form G116, the trip report, which can be submit-ted at leisure and so on.

Surprised? Not really. Manuals fit in to the comfort zone of most managers as it de-risks all decisions taken and does not put undue pressure on anyone to own responsibility.

Thus, we read about the IBM way, the GE way or the Ford way, the manuals of which dictate how the business ought to be run and the managers are evaluated based on how slavishly they follow such manuals.

No wonder then that even these giants have had to reinvent themselves once in a while, with new CEOs who threw out the old manuals and wrote fresh manuals.

Centres of Excellence

Most companies allowing the business to run the managers are those which have at the core of their success a centre of excellence which enabled them to dominate the industry.

These centres could have been in any one of the critical dis-ciplines which separate successful companies—product-ideation cells, design studios, formulation labs, manufacturing expertise, marketing flair, project and logistics management skills and con-sumer insight, to name a few.

Successful companies exploit the competitive strength arising from such centres of excellence rationally and profitably. They nurture such centres with an eye on the future and make necessary investments to maintain such centres as the keystones for future growth.

But over time, some of these centres of excellence so dominate management thinking that they attain the aura of a holy cow, never to be questioned. The managers running these centres become the new Brahmins, strutting around building empires for themselves and do everything possible to 'protect' the centre of excellence from the 'contamination of change'.

Unfortunately, a static centre of excellence will inevitably become a millstone around the organization's neck, and the organization, forced down by a path driven by internal logic, divorced from the reality of the market place, will begin its journey downhill.

Smart companies know this. They never abandon the core strength of a centre of excellence, but keep working on it, to ensure that it remains relevant.

Coca-Cola has retained its appeal through half a dozen generations since its introduction some 130 years ago. Over the years, the original Coke formulation has not changed much barring a minor tweak or two, but the packaging has, many times and even the delivery systems have evolved with Coke fountains contributing handsomely to Coca-Cola's overall market share.

Coca-Cola has emerged as the number one brand in soft drinks once its centre of excellence moved from the proprietary 'cure all' medicine category at its inception in 1886 to a strong customer focus—understanding of its customers, monitored through continuous research tracking purchase and consumption patterns of each family member, and its ability to quickly act on the research findings.

Thus, Coca-Cola has maintained its pre-eminence in the soft drink industry by responding to changes in consumer habits and attitudes by adding new formulations and flavours to cater to the emerging niche segments. The Coca-Cola company stable today has more than 400 brands and variants selling in 180 odd countries. Almost half of its business is in non-carbonated drinks.

Companies such as Coca-Cola, in which centres of excellence are customer led, meaning those who respond quickly to changing and evolving customer needs stay market leaders for the longest time.

In the United Kingdom, for example, brand leadership positions have not changed for almost a 100 years in markets as diverse as bread and vacuum cleaners.

Brand Leaders for 100 Years

Product Category	Premier Brands in 1920s and Now
Bread	Hovis
Soup	Heinz
Margarine	Stork
Cornflakes	Kellogg's
Chocolate Bars	Cadbury
Mixer Drinks	Schweppes
Toothpaste	Colgate
Tea	Brooke Bond
Vacuum Cleaners	Hoover

Source: Chanda (2010).[3]
Note: This is not an exhaustive list.

The preponderance of FMCG (fast moving consumer goods) brands in this list is not a surprise as FMCG companies (e.g., Unilever, P&G, Nestle, Johnson & Johnson and so on) had adopted a customer-led business model very early, evidenced by frequent new product launches and relaunches of successful products often embellished by the addition of variants. No shampoo brand, for example, will have less than two dozen variants and pack sizes on retail shelves at any point of time.

The surprise is Hoover, a company whose centre of excellence has evolved around its strength in technology, not as amenable to respond to changes in consumer needs and choice determinants as FMCG products which is amply illustrated by Kodak, another brand which would have featured in the above-mentioned list

---

[3] Chanda, Pradip. 2010. *A Requiem for a Brand*. New Delhi: Lotus Collection, Roli Books.

less than a decade ago, now consigned to nostalgia as the ubiquitous digital camera, a must-have feature even in the cheapest mobile phone, has made Kodak and its cameras and films totally redundant. I can actually sympathize with Kodak when it got caught between a rock and a hard place. As a virtual monopoly in the photo film business dependent on a century old camera technology, their eyes may not have dwelled too long on the digital phenomenon which would completely bypass the need for a film to record a picture or a studio to develop a print. And then before Kodak could blink, the venerated camera got pushed aside by a lowly upstart, a mobile phone.

The plight of Kodak puts in perspective the threats posed to companies whose centre of excellence is in technology.

Recently, Ford, with its centre of excellence lying in its expertise in making large 'gas guzzling' automobiles designed for an American market, which was increasingly switching to smaller, eco-friendlier autos, went into near-bankruptcy and were forced to introduce new engines and models to return to viability.

For Ford, it was a déjà vu moment as almost 80 years earlier a similar turnaround was required for *The Model T*.

Henry Ford, the founder of Ford Motor Co., celebrated his 60th birthday in 1923. The same year, Ford sold 57 per cent of all cars sold in America. With sales exceeding two million units, Ford accounted for almost half the sales of motor cars in the world.

Ford's phenomenal success was based on a no-nonsense, affordable, user-friendly car which virtually single-handedly brought about an automobile revolution in the United States—The Model T.

The early success of this mass-produced car is best appreciated by the car penetration figures in America after Ford entered the market.

Year	1902	1904	1905	1923
Cars Per Million People	66	154	1,250	2,5100

Ford's greatest strength was its 'low cost capability' assiduously built over a period of time, focusing primarily on productivity efficiencies. Ford was able to market a car at a very affordable price that brought hordes of new customers into the net every year.

Ford virtually pioneered a mass production revolution, built around the conveyer belt system, and eventually went on to build one of the largest production complexes of its time. The results were spectacular. In a little over a decade, the Ford factory was able to churn out a car every 10 seconds, some 4,500 times faster than when it started production.

Unfortunately, owing to the single-minded focus on efficient production, Henry Ford never developed a customer focus.

While the Model T remained a good value for money car, the tastes of the car buyer were rapidly changing. A car was no longer just a means to travel from point A to point B. It was now a statement about the owner, his aspirations and ambitions. And for the first time, his wife had a say in the selection of the car. Style and colours became important features, which the competition was exploiting to wean traditional Ford customers away.

But Ford continued to believe that people still buy cars only for convenience and as long as Ford was able to maintain its cost leadership, its dominance of the market was guaranteed. He refused to accept that with better standards of living, and more money to spend, customers were looking for value additions, a condition that competitors, notably General Motors, exploited cleverly.

Clearly, the blind faith in its centre of excellence was going to pull the business down.

Barely, three years after Ford's record sales, in May of 1927, all the Ford factories had to shut down to retool for the new model forced upon them by the market—the Model A.

Model A in due course did revive Ford's flagging market presence somewhat but the delay in recognizing market trends, and the resistance to introduce different models for the different customer segments that were emerging, cost Ford market its market leadership. Competition, notably General Motors, was given the time to establish their differentiation based on styling, and the Model A got relegated to an entry level car, to be jettisoned as soon as the owner was able to afford to buy a car with better features, smoother rides and attractive 'gadgets'.

Businesses Do Not Fail: People Do

This is a very popular refrain among union leaders, often justifiably so.

The ouster of the Ambassador car, dominating Indian roads till the late 1990s is a case in point.

Hindustan Motors (HM) set up a car manufacturing facility soon after 1947, as the dealerships of imported British and American cars wound down their businesses because of the scarcity of foreign currency, a common ailment in all markets after WWII.

The first car on the road was a Hindustan, soon followed by the Landmaster and then the Ambassador, a Morris Oxford look alike, all built on platforms acquired from Morris Motors of England.

The owner of HM reckoned that in the regulated economy prevailing in newly independent India, where production of all goods were limited to a few license holders—three for automobiles— the low purchasing power of the masses will limit car ownership to institutions, the government and government-owned/funded institutions being the largest of them. This perception fitted well with his company's 'environment management' skills, a euphemism for knowing the right people to get institutional orders.

An added bonus was the company's ability to pass cost escalations to the buyer in the absence of serious competition, as the other two license holders were constrained by capacity limitations. Thus, there was no pressure on the company to achieve better cost and performance efficiencies, which proved to be fatal in the long run.

HM had selected the model well. The Ambassador was a hardy car, with a strong chassis and a suspension system that could withstand the rough surfaces of Indian roads. It was roomy enough to accommodate large Indian families, and a large number of roadside mechanics found the engine of the car simple enough to cope with the not infrequent breakdowns. The Ambassador certainly provided a better ride than most buses for the passengers and driving comforts were designed for the low-paid driver, rather than the rare owner driver. The brakes worked well, so did the horn, the two essentials for highway driving in India. Another player, an India-made Fiat offered similar features but in a smaller body, and were forced to be content with a distant second position. Standard, the third player in the market was too small to matter.

In the early 1980s, paradoxically, it was a government joint venture which posed the first challenge to the Ambassador. It introduced a small car, Maruti 800, infinitely more customer friendly and fuel efficient, that appealed to a newly emerging middle class ready for self-ownership. Pent-up demand from this segment had been growing for some time and the Maruti fitted the requirement perfectly. A car financing scheme introduced by Maruti further increased its penetration among the individual owners.

The 1990s ushered deregulation in India, and by 1996 at least 16 international car majors had set up shop in India to cater to the new affluent middle class now ready to graduate to bigger models than the Maruti. Fortunately for Maruti, the international players focused on the nascent midsize car segment, a segment so far occupied by the Ambassador, leaving Maruti to lord it over the small car segment.

Ambassador lost ground rapidly and the company started making losses. HM's response? An advertisement assuring the customer that an Ambassador will not be an Ambassador if they change the shape!

It is not known as to why HM decided to continue with the Ambassador. Setting up new platforms to build cars is a capital-intensive affair. HM may not have had access to such funds.

Neither did they appear keen to explore other related business opportunities seriously. An attempt to market bulletproof cars for VIPs was made at one stage and they did market a Japanese sedan for a while. None of these initiatives could stem the mounting losses, and HM eventually had to shut shop.

Was there an opportunity lost?

Comfort in One's Zone

Far too many companies get too used to its comfort zone. They forget that comfort leads to complacency, which in turn makes the company too lethargic to keep an eye open both to threats and opportunities to grow.

When a company operates in a closed economy, a sense of comfort is inevitable. If you can't grow, neither can competition, so your position in the market is secure. Licenses to manufacture with capped capacities ensured that.

The two-wheeler, primarily scooters, market in India was another example of artificially created comfort zones. Some of the production licenses were for such absurdly low volumes, that a customer, having ordered a scooter with a down payment, often had to wait for six years for delivery!

The story was no different for cement or steel, toothpastes or washing powders, textiles or processed foods. Because along with the license, the manufacturer got a guaranteed share of the market, the consumer faced with dire shortages made do with whatever was available.

Efficient companies utilized licensed capacities fully in no time at all and got lulled into a sense of security, not the best of readiness when the environment changes and a licensed economy transforms into a free market economy.

The industry in India realized this in the early 1990s when suddenly all restrictions on production were lifted and simultaneously import restrictions on raw materials and components eased. With the volumes of end products low, the supply chain was limited too.

Companies, for the first time facing real competition, were shaken out of their comfort zones. But environment change takes a while to gather momentum, in this case long enough for some business houses to put a set of blinkers on and continue to believe that free market economy is not for real. Some industrialists did try to turn the clock back and brought pressure on the government to slow down, if not abandon, the free market orientation, till Indian companies are ready to face the new big villain, international competition. Their pleas remained unheeded.

Many, in fact too many, companies had become so used to the comfort zone, that they were far from ready to tackle this new menace. For the first time, owners and boards of companies had to ask the dreaded question—exit or turnaround?

CHAPTER 5

THE PERENNIAL DILEMMA
TURNAROUND OR EXIT

Life cycles of corporations have not changed much over the years.

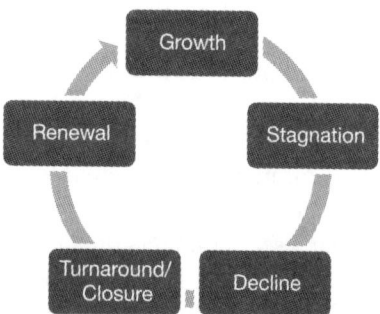

What has changed is that the windows of opportunity between stages are closing a lot faster. No longer are corporations guaranteed to have a few, in some cases a few decades, to enjoy the profits of the growth phase. Neither do corporations get much breathing time between realizing that they are actually stagnating and must initiate the 'second curve', before the slide accelerates to the dreaded fork—turnaround or closure.

Standing still in such a scenario is not an option available to the management of any corporation.

Retaining market share in an ever expanding market, competition becoming more intense with the entry of nimbler new players often with better and cheaper alternative solutions, is never easy.

Clocking some year-on-year topline growth, but at a rate lower than market growth for a year or two, may give a semblance of comfort to the top management especially if the bottom line growth is maintained. This, however, is a false paradise. The loud and clear message to anyone willing to listen is that the company is stagnating.

Because in such a scenario the bottom line growth can only be achieved by pruning of costs. Some flab is always available even in the best run companies, but such flab will be used up soon. Furthermore, pruning of costs will impact the corporation's ability to make investments on technology upgrade, development of new products and services, retention and retraining of its human capital and so on. In short, the corporation will no longer remain competitive. The slide downward towards the dreaded fork—turnaround or closure will only accelerate.

Economic logic dictates that when the return on investments becomes lower than the cost of capital, the entity is eroding shareholders' value. In such a situation, the entity should be sold as a going enterprise, if possible. If no buyer is forthcoming, the enterprise should be wound up, assets sold and the freed capital invested in more lucrative opportunities. In fact, many smart managers do take this step when the very first signs of declining profitability become evident.

Boards of large corporations, with multiple strategic business units (SBUs) or subsidiaries handling different businesses have to contemplate turnaround versus closure fairly routinely.

A subsidiary or an SBU may lag behind market growth or perform poorly vis-à-vis other SBUs/subsidiaries within the corporation and the board needs to convince itself of the long-term viability of such a unit. The board also needs to weigh the merits of deploying resources to turnaround an under-performing SBU/subsidiary with the surpluses of a healthier SBU/subsidiary.

Making a wrong decision may have a domino effect on the entire corporation. Ignoring a strong case to reinvest the surpluses of a healthy SBU in its own sphere of activity, so necessary to ensure continued competitiveness and retaining its market position is, at best, a very risky gamble, especially if the surplus is diverted to prop up an under-performing SBU/subsidiary.

The profitable SBU suddenly starved of required investments may end up on the brink of closure, that too very rapidly. A recent example of the dire consequences of such reckless diversion of surpluses from profit-making SBUs is the case of the UB Group, India. Keeping Kingfisher, a loss making and badly managed airline from day one, afloat with cross sister company funding within the group, eventually led to the ouster of the largest shareholder who was also the chairman of the group.

Decisions to divest or close non-performing SBUs are easier to make, as the traumas created by such moves can be contained within the group/corporation with minimal displacement, dislocation and depreciation of both physical and human resources.

The decision of the Tata Group to sell its steel-producing factories in the United Kingdom and Europe has been a popular topic in business journals and TV over the last few months.

To quote from The Economic Times of 31 March 2016, 'Tata Steel has decided to sell or restructure its poorly performing UK steel business, giving up its nine-year fight to salvage the operations of the business as part of the takeover of Corus at the height of the commodity price boom in 2007'.

The report further adds, 'The decision stoked a furor over jobs and business conditions in referendum-bound Britain and a smart rally in Tata Steel's share price' brilliantly articulating the stark divergence of sentiments between the two opposite end of the spectrum of the stakeholders.

The steel industry has always been known to go through regular boom and bust cycles. So much so that Peter Drucker had observed 50 odd years ago that the steel industry's fortunes are determined by wars; the more wars fought on the ground, the more is the demand for steel. Had he qualified wars with a prefix 'conventional', we could probably understand better the present bust cycle, given the number of 'wars' being fought against a multitude of terror groups.

The Tata Corus story began in 2004 when the then British Steel Chairman James Leng flew down to Bombay to see whether Tata would be interested in buying Corus.

Mr Leng must have been very aware of the cyclical vagaries of the steel business and therefore keen to exit during the boom time. The tragic interlude in early 1980s, when one of his predecessors Ian MacGregor had launched a drastic turnaround initiative, must have been deeply etched in the collective memory of the company. In the process of which, over five years, the company was almost decimated. Production capacity was halved to 14 million tons from a peak of 28 million tons, the workforce reduced to 52,000 from 265,000. All this after the government wrote off US$ 6 billion debt of the company and agreed to supply energy (a significant input cost in steel making) at subsidized rates.

Mr Leng must have been a very happy man when the Tata group, after some years of deliberation, agreed to buy Corus for US$ 7 billion. Mr Tata must have been equally delighted.

The proposal was a win–win for both companies. Tata Steel in India, stuck in bureaucratic wrangles for many years, in a bid to put up a 5 million tons plant in Odisha, was forced to scout for opportunities outside the country. Leng knew that Corus needed to secure raw material supply sources to survive another cyclical downturn of the industry. Tata would have been able to provide such security as well as bring in the funds required for technology upgradation.

Had a Brazilian cement-to-steel conglomerate not decided to put in counter bids, which eventually pushed the acquisition price tag to almost twice the earlier agreed price, it may have been a win–win situation for both.

The new price tag was certainly a big win for Corus shareholders but for Tata it turned out to be a millstone around its neck. Not only did the Tata group have to take an asset impairment charge of US$ 2.8 billion over five years due to poorly performing UK business, but also it has not been able to turn a profit since the takeover.

Had the acquisition gone through at the originally agreed price, this predicament—keep or sell—may have been put on the back burner for a while longer as the lower interest costs alone would have made Tata Steel UK look more viable till the next boom comes along.

One can only wonder why, when rational pursuit of economic interests determined US$ 7 billion as the fair price for the acquisition of Corus, did the Tata group get involved in a bidding war and ended up paying almost twice as much. Especially as the bid price was increasing only by 10 pence per share at a time, there were multiple opportunities to pull out.

The Tata group has never been known as an overly aggressive player in any of the 100 odd industry segments they are in. In many, they are the market leaders, but never the aggressors. So what motivated Tata to act so out of line with their own philosophy? Were they inspired by L.K. Mittal's heavily leveraged buyout of Arcelor? Being a steel man, Mr Tata would certainly have known about the periodic cycles of boom and bust this industry goes through. Estimating the yield 10 years hence in such a predictably cyclic industry would therefore have been a major gamble. So what non-economic motivation guided Ratan Tata's decision to acquire Corus at what seemed to be 'at any price'? We may never know.

Stand-alone Companies

For stand-alone businesses, an exit decision is entirely dependent on how a potential buyer values the enterprise. The best that the management can do is to make a list of companies which can see some value in acquiring an under-performing company to fit into their future plans and send discreet feelers to them. For a reasonable size company, this is best done through the intermediaries who specialize in mergers and acquisitions (M&A).

A smaller company, unable to hire the services of an M&A firm, will try for a takeover through an old boy network. If that does not happen, the only exit route is closure.

In a free economy, such as the United States, such a company will file for bankruptcy. A receiver will take over the task of dismantling the company. The steps are well documented: lay off the staff, monetizes all saleable assets, pay off lenders and other creditors first from the proceeds, rarely more than a few cents for every dollar owed, pay off all the lawyers involved, notify the concerned regulatory bodies and close the company.

Shareholders are left with the scrips which some keep as mementos, others consign them to the shredder. Employees will be lucky if they get some token redundancy cheques.

This process does not work too well in other countries. In many countries, both developed such as France and Germany, and developing such as India, corporate laws, especially labour laws, zealously safeguarded by militant unions, often with tacit support from governments make closures almost impossible.

It works in the United States, because over time, workers and their unions have acknowledged that the established social support systems do cushion the hardships of retrenched employees following closures for some time, often long enough to find alternative employment. Hence, unviable companies are not forced to keep factory gates open, only to keep people on the payroll.

The macro perspective is equally clear—assets, released from the liquidation of a non-performing company, deployed in a new venture keeps the overall balance intact. Even if the new venture is located somewhere else, economists argue that such a dislocation will only cause 'local pain'. Both capital and the workforce are highly mobile, hence such local pain is only a short-term inconvenience.

But, the closure of a large unit of a company can have devastating effects on the community it abandons. It has been well documented in a number of cases.

Robert Shook wrote in his book *Turnaround: The New Ford Motor Company*[1] almost three decades ago:

> Ford plants were often the largest employers in their communities. Closing these plants was catastrophic to many areas. A huge number of workers flooded the local job markets making it impossible to provide work for all the unemployed. Those who got hired were apt to settle for a smaller salary. The local economy

---

[1] Shook, Robert. 1990. Turnaround: The New Ford Motor Company. Prentice Hall Trade.

is destroyed as the reduction in spending ruins many small shop-keepers and service-related businesses. The ensuing massive exile of workers, who are forced to relocate, causes the value of local real estate to plummet. Sellers are forced to take losses on their homes, wiping out any equity they may have accumulated over the years.

To a worker it inflicts anguish, humiliation, and financial hardship. An entire family is victimized. The side effects often include increased rates of alcoholism, wife and child abuse, and suicide.

In a macabre replay, we read about the destruction of Detroit, the world's undisputed auto capital since the introduction of cars at the turn of the 20th century, and the effects on the community depending on these corporations for a living, again in 2008.

'Once the capital of the U.S. auto industry, which almost single-handedly helped to create the American middle-class, Detroit has been crippled by the closing of factories, falling home prices, the exodus of tens of thousands of residents, rampant violent crime and massive poverty'.[2]

This explains why turnaround attempts have to be made. Some companies are too big to be allowed to fail because of the collateral damage such failures bring in their wake.

The 2008 US government multibillion dollar bailout to keep auto majors, insurance biggies, bank titans and mortgage companies afloat is a case in point. We can only imagine the magnitude of the depression that would have followed if any one of General Motors, Ford, AIG or Fannie Mae was allowed to fold up.

Over time, governments have stepped in to prop up companies too big to fail in almost all countries. Railways, shipping, utility, steel, textile, jute, insurance, banking, virtually every industry you can think of has received massive bailouts, and when these failed to revive the ailing companies, many of them were nationalized.

Steel Authority of India comprises many ailing public and private sector steel companies. Similarly, Shipping Corporation of India and Jute Corporation of India have provided succour to

---

2 Ghosh, Palash. May, 2011. IB Times.

many companies in distress. British Rail was also the refuge for many loss-making private railroads for almost four decades after World War II, till these were privatized again.

In the process, some absurd government bailout/acquisitions have also happened.

Some years ago, a colleague and I held a two-day workshop for the CEOs of 26 ailing engineering companies all acquired by the government of West Bengal. We were shocked to discover that none of these companies were receiving any working capital to attempt any kind of revival. But the monthly payroll for the employees, a few thousands, was met without demur. Appropriately enough, the workshop was being held at The Great Eastern Hotel, once a landmark in Kolkata, another private enterprise taken over by the government!

Believe it or not, even Modern Bakery in Delhi was taken over by the government at one stage. Fortunately, it has been reprivatized.

What about smaller companies? Can the owners/managers cut their losses, close the company, sell the saleable assets and start over?

If it is an equity-funded company, the answer is probably yes, but most companies in India, of some size have a debt equity ratio often in excess of 3:1.

In such scenarios, the largest block of 'stakeholders', that is, the small shareholders rarely have a voice. They are totally dependent on the management's call on closure or exit.

Then whose narrow interests will be served by attempting a turnaround? If you really think about it, the interest of the lenders, primarily those of the consortium of lending banks, mostly public sector unit (PSU) banks assume primacy, and the owner/managers end up working for them.

These banks, often charged with crony capitalism, do over extend their exposure by sanctioning loans without due diligence, perhaps swayed by the charisma of the entrepreneur who is judged by not what he knows but who he knows. Come crunch time the banks want their pound of flesh, by way of repayment of the loan—principal, accumulated unpaid interest, compounded by penal interest on unpaid interest—before giving a nod to closure. They can call the shots, because all the saleable assets of the distressed company are not only hypothecated as collateral to these banks, but may even have second charge on the same assets given to other creditors. To cap it all, often the owner/directors are required to provide personal guarantees as further collateral and are vulnerable to legal action which may stretch to jail terms.

The owner/manager has no option but to try an attempt a revival, egged on by the lenders, at times threatened by takeover of management control.

Other stakeholders, the sundry creditors, such as vendors and service providers, have little clout, though at times very large vendors do actually continue the supply chain, hoping that the company will be able to eventually turnaround and square up their debts. In fact, many airlines and shipping companies have been bailed out by such creditors. In some instances, vendors go the extra mile to take over the distressed company and manage to turn these around.

The next group of stakeholders which can influence the decision comprises the workers, and their unions who, as we have witnessed many times, are capable of violent and destructive protests. In India, these stakeholders are further encouraged by the attitude of the government, who put enormous pressure on owners and managers of even small and midsized companies to avoid closures. True, some state governments have amended labour laws to permit closure of very small units, employing less than 100 people. But exit remains elusive as the mandated severance packages are far too high, taxing the very limited resources of an ailing company, forcing the company management to limp along.

These stakeholders effectively trump the primary stakeholders, who, I submit, are the owners of the controlling shares, the owner.

The Indian Business Milieu

PSUs, multi-national companies (MNCs) and family-owned companies make up the medium to large segments in the Indian business milieu.

In the days, soon after India became independent, when the private capital market was small, the government stepped in to set up heavy industries, infrastructure building, power generation and many other essential businesses as the sole owner. Different PSUs were set up to run different units, managed by an IAS officer, a jack of all trades by training, as chairman.

In time, some of these PSUs were asked to take over many ailing companies and become one very large 'under-performing' unit. SAIL, National Textile Corporation Limited, Jute Corporation of India, Shipping Corporation of India, Mazagaon Dock Ltd and State Bank of India are a few examples of PSUs who had to acquire large family-run businesses under duress.

Strangely enough, most such PSUs follow the principle of protecting the 'family silver', at times with more ardour than some of the Harvard- or Yale-educated scions of family businesses do! These PSUs are political creations and turnaround or exit question has to be answered by the political bosses of the PSU chairmen. And only such bosses can understand why a state-owned airline needs to be kept alive at substantial cost to the tax payer.

MNCs tunes are created and orchestrated on foreign soil and exit is more top-of-mind for them than risky turnaround attempts for faltering businesses.

With the exception of a handful of 'first-generation owner managed' companies in telecom, entertainment, IT and now e-tailing, most other family-owned companies are now run by the second or third generations of the founder/owner. The only exception I can think of is Larsen & Toubro, where the management had been passed over to professional managers, who had no significant shareholding in the company.

Family businesses are by definition the traditional businesses they are in, and a matter of great pride to the owners. The very thought of exiting such businesses is anathema to the present generation running the business, irrespective of the continued viability of such a business. They may venture out into other businesses, which become the mainstay of the family's clutch of companies, but loyalty to the inheritance remains. For them, the answer to the question turnaround or exit is always turnaround.

The owner of the family business is the one who has the passion and zeal for the business and appoints the board, the chairman and the senior management team. Often the owner is also the chairman and CEO of the business.

The successful owners are those who are able to infuse the same passion and zeal among the senior management team, who in turn invest time and effort and emotional capital to succeed in the business.

The owners have different perspectives from the small investors with a few shares who show their loss of faith in the company by selling their shares and invest their monies elsewhere.

They have to, as they have made substantial investments of money, time, commitment and effort into the company over the years, and often go on a limb to guarantee repayment of loans taken by the business, in the growth phase.

At times, the owner is neither inclined to run the business nor able to. This rarely happens when the first generation owner is still alive and able. It's largely a third or fourth generation phenomenon, at least in the United States and the United Kingdom.

At such junctures, professional managers are brought in, but the mandate remains clear—no exit. Yes, the managers get paid, often handsomely, but fortunately often managers come on board for the challenge and not for the money. Self-actualization derived from the satisfaction of a job well done is the prime motivator for the manager. How else would we explain why a Lee Iacocca, a Steve Jobs or a Narayanmurthy takes on tough turnaround assignments for token 'salaries', the equivalent of a US Dollar a year to be precise?

If we now go back to the two cases presented in Chapters 2 and 3, we may begin to better understand the imperatives of turnaround.

BFT was not in 'dire' straits. True, it had accumulated some losses, but it was close to a break-even point and the 'losses' were not mounting up. That apart it had no major borrowings from the banks. If it needed to raise a small loan to tide over a couple of bad business months, the owner was both able and willing to advance such loans.

Neither did BFT have a large unionized direct workforce who could have forced it to stay in the business. Nor did it have a list of creditors breathing down its neck to clear past dues.

So why did it embark upon a revival journey? It was the passion of the owner to keep a family legacy alive and leave for posterity a thriving heritage for the next two generations. It had to be a 'successful' company for the next generation to remain interested, and success in a business is measured by the bottom line.

As good a reason as any to attempt a revival, many other enterprises are still open precisely because of this—the owner's passion for the business and the refusal to give into external pressure to close shutters.

As explained in Chapter 2, HMV was a classic basket case. The new owners agreed to take it over because the chairman was personally very fond of Indian music and was under pressure from the local government to save a company, an institution really, which pioneered the preservation of the country's rich musical heritage. Having taken the company over, exit was obviously no longer an option, without giving a revival attempt a good, honest try.

Who should then lead the turnaround? The earlier management had failed either to anticipate or prepare themselves to tackle technical obsolescence and rampant piracy, the two most potent threats to the company's survival.

As we have seen in an earlier chapter, destructive changes in the market place, driving companies to the brink of closure, do not happen overnight. Such crises creep on to only those who choose not to take the winds of change seriously, and continue with the same product portfolio and business model, hoping that the good old days will come back.

This of course never happens.

Ergo, the present management, especially the CEO, must be made accountable, and forced to hand over charge to new change agents, who will bring in fresh perspectives, the will and the energy to lead the turnaround effort.

A Recap

When a decision to attempt a turnaround is thrust upon a company, the odds are stacked up against it.

To begin with, resources, or rather lack of resources, dictate the options available to the turnaround manager. Long-term strategy options may, with luck, evolve over time, but only after the company is nursed out of the present crisis.

Not having adequate working capital is the biggest crisis facing the turnaround manager.

Under-utilized assets are often the sole cash-generating source available to the company, and all short-term efforts have to focus on generating revenue through innovative asset utilization. Selling off assets is never the answer.

Generating a revenue stream to meet day-to-day expenses is not a goal by itself. The revenue is needed to mount a renewal process, which will give the turnaround manager some breathing space to formulate a sustainable strategy for long-term profitability and growth. It will also allow him to firm up on the winning business model.

CHAPTER 6

THE JOURNEY BEGINS
WHAT BUSINESS ARE WE IN?

Peter Drucker urges all CEOs to ask two questions at the beginning of each year:

1. What business are we in?
2. Should we stay in this business?

The natural follow up to the second question is: if we decide to stay in the business shall we continue with the same business model?

A turnaround manager normally comes on board only after the owner/board of the distressed company has explored other options, namely, exit via a merger/acquisition or closure. The remit given to him/her is clear. Stay in the business and make it viable.

Is it then too late for the turnaround manager to ask these questions? Wouldn't this be a waste of time? Shouldn't he/she roll up the sleeves and get down to some solid work, check expense vouchers, keep a tab on late comers, have meetings with managers and more meetings? Shouldn't cost reduction become the core focus?

In my mind, the answer is clear. Unless the new manager focuses on understanding the business he/she is expected to revive, no meaningful strategy and plan to go forward will emerge.

Chances of a turnaround attempt succeeding are the highest if the company can find a viable slot in the same business space it has been in.

Some knowledge of the market, its structure and nuances are known. Some relevant capabilities still exist. Some assets are still valuable. The order book is not totally blank. Some customers continue to be supportive. It is easier to come up with a game plan for the short term in such a scenario.

This game plan is not to be confused with a vision statement, which by definition is (a) long term, (b) it assumes a stable environment and (c) it presumes the company has the resources available to pursue the vision.

The aim of the immediate game plan is to demonstrate to everyone in the company that there indeed is a path forward, even though it may focus only on one or two areas—bolstering an existing revenue stream or still better, creating a new revenue stream, and, second, getting everybody, *every employee* in the company to engage in some productive activity. Successful execution of such an action plan, gets everyone to believe that there indeed is a path forward, and energizes the whole company to put their shoulders behind whatever efforts are made to the company back on its feet.

Once some semblance of a rehabilitation programme is under way, the turnaround CEO gets some breathing time to revisit the question of a 'what business are we in?' The more appropriate question perhaps is, 'what is the core of our business?' A vision for the company evolves from the answer you get from this question and becomes the guiding star for future growth.

There are zillions of words written on how to define what business a company is in.

What Business Are We in?

Visionary buggy manufacturers have successfully argued that they are in the transportation business and have gone on to make cars, trucks and aircrafts, launched car hire companies and even provided pick up and drop commuter services to call centres.

The buggy whip manufacturer may have had similar illusions but would have found that the jump from making whips to motor cars is a leap too far.

As markets develop and grow in size, defining the business becomes that much more difficult, as it is no longer a broad brush stroke but a far more chiselled analysis of the market structure and segmentation.

'We are in the transportation business' is easy to say but Rolls-Royce sees its market very differently from a company owning oil tankers, or say Indian Railways or Amtrak. Even within the automobile market, Rolls-Royce's perspective of the market will be vastly different from that of the mandarins at Suzuki house.

Soon after the introduction of automobiles in the early 1900s, there were two ways to look at the industry.

One was to see automobiles as a luxury item meant only for the super rich. The other was to see this as a desirable step up from bicycles, buggies and other uncomfortable modes of transport for those who are not blessed with large inheritances or sizeable pay packets.

Those who saw this as a toy for the rich, focused on smooth rides, handcrafted saloons, plush seats, built-in bars, state-of-the-art music systems and a host of 'non-essential' accessories. Rolls-Royce, Daimler AG and Mercedes-Benz saw the market developing this way, and made their products accordingly, setting luxury standards for themselves to be bettered only by themselves. Rolls-Royce remains the gold standard in luxury cars even today, with queens, kings and emirs their perennial patrons. Only modesty prevents heads of many other states to settle for a Mercedes.

Henry Ford saw it very differently. He saw the vast opportunity in being able to put every man (he wasn't a feminist) at the controls of a four-wheel motorized vehicle. The only obstacle he saw in his path was the cost of the car, too prohibitive for the pocket of the average American.

Ford decided to set it right. First, he focused on bringing down the cost of producing a car, which would enable him to reduce the prices of cars. And then he created a new market segment by putting more money in the workers' pocket.

Ford was totally enamoured by Frederick Winslow Taylor's modern idea of production—break each function down into much smaller units, so that each could be mechanized and speeded up and eventually flow into a straight-line production of little pieces becoming steadily larger.

The flywheel magneto was the first item to be produced on such an assembly line. The magneto assembly was broken up in 29 different operations and performed by 29 different men, halving the time taken to produce a magneto.

The assembly line production process was then extended to other components and parts. The result was a dramatic reduction in production time, more output per worker hour, and a virtual elimination of assembly line errors and the need to rework. The car's quality and reliability vastly improved because of the process changes.

In sum, Ford was able to make a better car at a lower cost. Passing the cost savings to the customer was a no-brainer thereafter. The ex-showroom price of a Model T was US$ 780 in 1910. In 1916, it was rolling out at US$ 360, at less than half of the 1910 price!

Ford then proceeded to hike up the wages of his workers to $5, yes five dollars a day, double the going wages, which forced other companies also hike their wages, thus putting additional money in many thousands of pockets to line up and buy a Ford Model T.

Ford was ready to go laughing to the bank as he had prepared to meet the demand surge—a phenomenon he had created—he now had the production capacity to sell as many cars as all his competitors put together.

Ford, writes David Halberstam in his seminal book *The Reckoning*, was so frustrated with the 380 per cent turnover of the labour force in 1913, the year of the great mechanization, that he figured he must do something radical to retain his trained workers, like doubling their wages. It seems that Ford firmly believed that it was a mistake to spend money on the finest machinery and then put those machines in the hands of 'disgruntled, unreliable, perhaps incompetent men'.

Ford later insisted that this was the best cost-cutting move he ever made. Justifiably so, it would appear. The public goodwill this move created was so great that Ford was able to cut back on his advertisement and promotional expenses even when sales of his Model T were soaring to such an extent that Ford's profits jumped from US$20 million in 1914 to US$60 million in 1915.

Then in the 1920s, Alfred Sloan, the chairman of General Motors, sliced and diced the vast market between a Ford and a Rolls in so many segments, that it became even more difficult to define 'the business we are in'.

Ford was driven by his conviction that low-cost capability is the key to success, and consequently maintained his focus on the more price sensitive 'entry level' car segment. Ford's passion for production efficiency—high speed and low cost—pushed him to eventually set up the Rouge, often described as an independent industrial city state; 1,100 acres, a mile and a half long and three quarters of a mile wide, contained 93 buildings. There were 93 miles of railroad track on it and 27 miles of conveyer belts, as well as a steel and a glass plant.

'The process was,revolutionary. On Monday morning, a barge bearing ore would arrive in a ship, the ore would go into a blast furnace. By Tuesday morning, it would be poured into a foundry mold and later that day would become an engine'. All this in 1924!

This plant came in very handy when Ford had to stop producing the Model T some years later, and launch the Model A.

Segmentation and product differentiation, each presenting a stand-alone 'business opportunity' exists in all industries.

In keeping with the Japanese acumen for miniaturization, Canon had developed a table top photocopying machine. Unable to compete with Xerox in the large volume copying needs of the corporate offices, Canon exploited an untapped segment of the market—small businesses that needed to make small numbers of copies of documents. These businesses were too small to attract the aggressive Xerox sales guys to make a pitch for their 'rent a machine and pay per copy' model. Canon dominated this market for many years.

GE, the world leader in manufacturing a large range of medical equipment, found itself in a peculiar predicament when they tried to tap markets outside the United States and Europe. The GE 'Hospital' model of the ultra-sound machine, for example, was too expensive for many developing markets, and its penetration was restricted to a small number of large well-funded hospitals.

GE responded by developing a small portable ultra sound machine which in turn spawned a new market segment in GE's non-traditional markets.

Such low-cost devices allowed the growth of a number of small mom-and-pop diagnostic centres, to offer a variety of services at very affordable prices to a large number of 'needy' patients, *immediately*.

The impact of this can best be gauged by a short anecdote.

When my brother-in-law, who lives in the United Kingdom, needed an ultrasound of his prostate gland, he was informed by the nearest NHI hospital that the earliest the ultrasound can be scheduled was 12 weeks away.

In India, if my general practitioner (GP) wants me to get an ultrasound done, all I have to do is walk 800 metres to the nearest shopping centre and pick any one of three or four clinics, nestling among small grocers, hairdressers, laundries and miscellaneous shops, with trained technicians or even doctors in attendance. I can be back home with the detailed printouts within the hour. Of course I have to pay for this service, a few US dollars equivalent. But the complications caused by a 12-week delay in detection of enlargement/infection of my prostate, I am sure, would have cost me very much more.

There are now inexpensive self-administered gadgets to measure blood sugar levels, blood pressure and so on. There are also portable electrocardiography (ECG) machines with attached printers carried by medical insurance company doctors when they come for a health check before issuing a policy.

Can you see the dilemma a medical equipment manufacturer faces when he/she had to determine 'what business am I in?' How do I define my universe? Big multi-specialty hospitals or local collection centres of pathology labs?

In BFT, the question was settled by their manufacturing process, very difficult to scale up because every tile was handcrafted. Either it opted to become a Rolls among flooring tiles or shut shop.

In HMV India, it was more complex.

In the United States or United Kingdom, various companies and labels, tend to focus on specific genres. Motown, was the mecca for jazz artists in the United States. Virgin in the United Kingdom was the hip label for the pop bands, whereas EMI straddled all genres with older artists filling up their roster.

In India, however, the relatively high cost of capital in setting up a professional sound recording studio and vinyl record pressing plant, made Gramophone & Typewriters Company, better known as HMV, the subsidiary of soon to be EMI Music, a virtual monopoly, since it started its operations in 1902. True, a couple of other record pressing plants came up later, but their capacities were too small to matter.

To add insult to injury, since records were the only form of 'packaged' music (I know it sounds crude), artists flocked to EMI for recording their repertoire. No point in singing your heart out if the connoisseur cannot take it home, is there?

By default, HMV became the repository of Indian music—all genres, all languages, almost all artists—including film sound tracks, which needed the records to promote their film. Incidentally, the government-owned radio stations only used records to play their music. Who supplied the records? HMV of course.

You can't quite blame the HMV managers for believing that they were in 'the business of producing records', can you?

So when the crunch came, with cassettes making their debut, HMV tried to protect their business, 'making records', forgetting that their business was to propagate recorded music, whatever be the medium.

As we have seen in the HMV case, the realization that HMV was in the business of creating content—recording and propagating music, *and not making records or cassettes*, was the crucial first step in defining the way forward. HMV in the process learnt how to tackle future disruption in the technology of delivering music to the customer.

One of the most talked about turnarounds in recent times is that of Ford when Mulally, a non-industry man was brought in to do the job.

Imagine Alan Mulally at Ford spending time mulling over these questions in 2007.

Not only would his management team be bewildered, but so would be the shareholders and of course *Wall Street*. Everyone knows that Ford makes cars, and more often than not, make a lot of money in the process. Of course they are in the 'business of making cars' and must continue to make cars and strive to win back their market share. Mulally had to accept this as a mandate.

Should We Stay in the Business?

Being a turnaround veteran, Mulally knew that when any market becomes very large and fragmented like the automobile market, the problem is to define the segment which you can make 'the business you are in'. Even General Motors, the pioneers in creating market segments and having models in many segments, could not straddle the entire market.

Mulally took a few critical decisions impacting the definition of 'what business are we in?'

Needing to act fast, Mulally's first major decision was to *better utilize Ford's primary asset—expertise in building traditionally fuelled cars*—but with a new stable of high performance and fuel-efficient cars with EcoBoost engines, which guzzled less gas and were demonstrably cheaper to run, a concept more appealing to the customer, who had become very conscious of the environment, specifically the harmful impact of emissions linked in turn to large gas guzzling cars, and was looking for more 'green' cars.

It would appear that a shift to customer focus needed to be spelt out because Ford was continuing to make cars owing to internal compulsions. The Ford plants were kept running making dated models because (a) the all-powerful union would not allow lay-offs and (b) the equally powerful accountants would not release funds for model upgradations requiring major retooling. Retooling meant investment and the accountants preferred to preserve cash, despite sitting on a seven-billion-dollar mountain of cash, a common enough anxiety in companies heading towards distress.

Consequently, *the inventory of unsold cars piled up and of course operational losses kept mounting.*

Another major strategy insight was that bigger is not necessarily better. This meant cutting production to match the real demand for the company's cars and trucks. The volume 'sacrifice' was compensated by making Ford vehicles so competitive that they could command a premium price and earn more for each vehicle sold.

By taking out excess capacity and increasing margins, Mulally was able to deliver record profits at a time when automobile sales were at historically low levels.

His turnaround recipe also included a major culture shift initiative. Mulally's chosen method to communicate these decisions to his managers, and get buy-ins from all stakeholders was to hammer home a process driven orientation—clearly define tasks ahead, and fix accountabilities in a manner that made cross-divisional and cross-departmental co-operation essential, the cornerstone of which was a weekly business process review meeting where attendance from all unit heads was a must. This was revolutionary in Ford's context, where unit bosses preferred to work in independent silos and rarely had the opportunity to look at the company as one seamless entity.

Is the Business Model Still Relevant?

The business model that the stressed company has been following is unlikely to have been very different from the other companies in the same market. Some of these other companies are not floundering. In fact, a few are making boatloads of money. So nothing can be very wrong with the business model.

Is it because other companies have been engaged in steadily responding to newer demands in the industry and the market by introducing changes to their business model frequently? Perhaps their changes were incremental, not radical enough to attract your attention, but effective enough to reach out to their customers and keep them happy.

Chances are that the competitors have been also busy in streamlining their business processes and fine-tuning data-based decision-making utilizing the myriad IT tools available to gather and analyze information and dramatically reduce their response for action time by keeping everyone in the loop through digitally managed communication and control systems. Similarly, customer communication is also real time, via social networks, e-mails and other digital contact tools. A reformulated product can now be introduced in a matter of minutes, instead of having to run expensive and time-consuming TV and other mass media advertising campaigns.

So why is your company in distress? The answer requires a close scrutiny of the components of the business model: the consumer profile, the product, the positioning, the price, the distribution channel, customer relationship management, human resource management, all these and more.

Many companies driven out of major markets by new products and services have found opportunities in new geographies. This is particularly true in developing markets where the impact of development economies is first felt in major cities and towns, and the trickle down impact to smaller towns and villages takes time, sometimes years.

The new geographies pose different challenges especially in management of logistics—getting the product to the consumer, and may require a complete relook at the product, packaging, unit pricing and the distribution process.

An oft-quoted success story in increasing penetration of high-value toiletries in India is the introduction of single-use shampoo sachets, to cater to the lower income group consumer segments where the high unit price of a conventional bottle was a major inhibitor to purchase.

In the FMCG industry, the product is king. There are a number of products which have dominated their market segments for ages because of their product formulation, for example, Crest toothpaste, Black Label whisky, Ribena health drink, Tabasco sauce, Ferrero Rocher Chocolates and of course Coca-Cola.

Coca-Cola reportedly had not changed its formulation since the summer of 1886 when it was launched, other than removing cocaine traces from the Coca leaves.

In the late 1980s, the picture was not looking too rosy for Coca-Cola in the United States. Market share had been shrinking steadily from 60 per cent in the 1950s to less than 24 per cent by 1983, largely because Pepsi was besting it in the 'cola wars', with consumers preferring Pepsi over Coke in 'blind tests'.

In 1985, exactly 99 years after Coke was launched, the management decided to reformulate the product, as a defensive measure.

This move created such uproar among loyal drinkers that Coke was forced to bring the original formulation back as Coke Classic within days of its withdrawal from the market.

'Yes, it infuriated the public', admitted Sergio Zyman, VP, marketing, a decade later, 'cost a ton of money and lasted only 77 days before we reintroduced Coca-Cola Classic. Still, new Coke was a success because it revitalized the brand and reattached the public to Coke'.

Coke had to re-learn the lesson 'Product is King' many years later in a different market.

When Coke re-entered the Indian market in 1990s, some 20 years after it had exited the market owing to government interference, it found a ready re-entry platform by way of acquiring Parle Soft Drinks, the largest indigenous soft drinks maker, who opted for discretion over valour and sold most of its business and brands to Coca-Cola. Coke's primary interest in Parle was its bottling plants and the national distribution infrastructure.

Along with the acquisition came Thums Up, the indigenous brand of Coca-Cola which had made Parle a household name.

The new Coca-Cola India management was clear in its mind that its primary task was to re-establish Coke as the number one soft drink in the country. The much publicized decision was to stop all support to Thums Up, making way for its withdrawal as soon as the existing inventory of Thums Up bottles is exhausted. The management was not too concerned about losing users—after all, the 'real thing' was making a grand re-entry and Coke should win over Thums Up, the copycat, drinkers in no time.

But much to the embarrassment of the Coca-Cola management, Thums Up refused to die. The Thums Up users made their preference for their favourite drink so loud and clear that the bottlers refused to stop bottling and selling Thums Up. Almost 20 years after Coke re-entered India, Thums Up remains the top selling drink in the Coke stable, and of course the number one Cola brand.

Despite such precedents, most product and R&D managers are often tempted to tinker with the product formulation, to be able to maintain margins as competition prevents price increase to offset cost escalations.

Take the case of a brand/product manager handling a brand of toothpaste which is chugging along, holding on to a high but steady market share in a moderately growing market.

How does the product manager show an increase in profits? Cutting costs of course.

A powwow with the R&D team reveals once again that the flavour is costing a pile. These French perfumers are real bandits. What to do? Can we risk switching to a lower cost local substitute that R&D has developed? Let's do a blind product test and see how the consumer reacts to the new flavour.

In due course, the product test results come in. Original is preferred but the consumer preference, says the market research company is not 'statistically significant'. So, of course batches start rolling out with the new lower cost flavouring agent.

Odd comments come in from the market, via the reps, but not taken too seriously. We know that consumers prefer the original, but the preference was not 'statistically significant'. Consumers will get used to it. They always do.

Another brand sniffs an opportunity and starts a major promotional campaign. The company's household panel research shows a marginal decline in the repeat purchase rate (RPR) of its toothpaste. The product manager ascribes this to the success of the competitor's promotional campaign. He ups the advertising budget putting the profitability of the brand under greater pressure. But surprisingly, the RPR drops again the next month, and the month after.

The MD gets upset and orders reinstitution of the original flavour. By the time the original flavour batches get to the market, a further few points have been eroded from the market share and the reducing RPRs are causing alarm.

The business model did not change. A 'statistically insignificant' tweak in the formulation was made. And lo and behold the brand is slipping into a coma.

The market can be so irrationally unforgiving, avers the ex-product manager in his next job interview.

Did he overlook an opportunity to test the wider acceptance of the new formulation, without putting the mother brand under threat, by way of a low cost digital launch of a 'variant' possibly at a lower price?

What the toothpaste example highlights is the lurking danger behind cost-cutting as a prime motive in any business.

As many turnaround experts focus on cost-cutting as their preferred strategy initiative, let us now look at the strategy options available to the turnaround manager.

The real challenge comes when a turnaround CEO finds that the company does not any longer have competitive strengths left to remain in the 'business' it was traditionally in.

Similarly, HM found out the same thing when Maruti was launched in the market, and soon international auto majors stepped in with far better cars.

In the 1990s, many Indian companies in diverse industries found themselves in the HM predicament.

Faced with the entry of Japanese, Korean and American brands selling white goods—air conditioners, washing machines, refrigerators, microwave ovens and so on—and electronic entertainment hardware such as TVs, music systems and DVD players, many Indian companies with inferior technology, were forced to exit. Some, Kelvinator and Allwyn among them, were fortunate enough to sell some of their assets—production facilities and access to a large dealer network—to the new MNCs, Sony, LG, Samsung, Toshiba and Whirlpool. A few others became third-party manufacturers and original equipment manufacturer (OEM) suppliers to the new market leaders.

I, however, submit that if you are either sitting or contemplating sitting on the hot seat of a turnaround manager, you must begin by seeking the answers to the three Drucker questions. The purpose of finding answers to these questions is not to better understand why the company has gone into a decline—when you are sitting on the hot seat. This is of academic interest.

The real purpose is to find the residual strengths—assets; the company still has to embark on a successful turnaround initiative.

These assets are not to be confused with the assets shown in the balance sheet of the company, which only reflect the residual monetary value of assets in 'conventional usage'.

All turnaround managers usually inherit a huge resource crunch along with their hot seat. Paucity of resources, especially cash, will soon convince the turnaround manager that the *only available path forward is to adopt renewal strategies dictated by an asset utilization philosophy—creative utilization of assets outside of their conventional application.*

This can actually be a boon in disguise. It will certainly stretch the turnaround managers' lateral thinking skills, especially if the company in distress has large legacy assets and a sizeable workforce, which if not gainfully employed, will pull the company down.

Not having cash to spare, the company will not be able to afford a rightsizing programme requiring expensive voluntary retirement schemes, and the payroll of the idle workforce alone will drag the company into oblivion. If only some of the idle workforce could be gainfully re-employed.

Let me leave you with an anecdote of a 'clever' strategy which never saw the light of day.

Many years ago, I was involved with a company with a large idle workforce. As it so happens the company was part of a group who also owned a utility company, generating thermal power and owning an exclusive power distribution license in a large city.

Those were the days of chronic power shortages in India. The utility company was unable to supply power 24/7 and was much maligned as a result. To make matters worse, a lot of power generated was wasted at low-demand hours, as the company's unit produced electricity at one standard rate irrespective of use.

These were also the early days of the inverter. An inverter, connected to the electric circuitry in an apartment, draws power from a fixed AC source, typically power received from a local power distribution company, and uses electronic circuitry to 'invert' AC power into DC power, which is then stored by charging one or two car batteries. In the event the main power supply trips, the inverter gets activated to reconvert the stored power into AC, and supplies power to run lights, fans, TVs, desktops and small appliances.

Some small entrepreneurs, inspired by Japanese companies had started selling inverters in the country, which were in great demand, especially in those cities where utility companies did not have adequate capacity, like the one I am talking about.

I floated a proposal to the chairman of the group.

Let the utility company convert each power buying home unit into a power store, at off-peak hours, by providing them with inverters and batteries, at a cost recoverable in say six months through monthly instalments. If the utility company is willing to provide the know-how to make the inverters, my idle workforce can be used to manufacture these.

It sounded like a win–win situation to me. My idle workforce becomes a revenue earner. The utility company earns consumer approbation for proactively reducing their misery, and in the process monetizing some of the wasted power generated. What we needed to do was rope in a car battery maker. As luck would have it there was one such company in India owned by a close relative of the group chairman.

The chairman approved the plan. But the bureaucrats at the utility company balked.

Such is life.

CHAPTER 7

THE BUILDING BLOCKS
UNLOCKING THE VALUE OF UNDER-UTILIZED ASSETS

Conventional wisdom says, like all other business initiatives, any turnaround journey must begin with a strategy. All strategies evolve from a focused vision and mission. Ergo, the process must begin with defining the vision. Right? In theory, yes, in practice, no.

Lou Gerstner, having taken on the challenge to steer IBM out of trouble, earned the scorn of business scribes, when he stated in his first press conference 'the last thing we need now is a vision'.

Having been in a similar position, I empathized with Mr Gerstner. The turnaround manager, more often than not, is new to the company, at times new to the industry as well. No matter how extensively he/she is briefed prior to taking on the hot seat, the new manager will need to spend some time in understanding the business and the company's position in the market and get a feel of what residual strengths can be used to build a turnaround platform.

Understanding the business begins with understanding the core of the company's business and an assessment of the full potential of the basic business. Most turnaround managers assume that the previous management had exploited fully the potential of the company's business. Despite that the company is in deep red. Hence, the core business must be nearing the end of its life cycle.

In the HMV story, we see the error in this logic. Content creation/ acquisition is the core business of any music company. Monetizing the content, via records, cassettes, compact discs, ring tones of phones or any other means is merely a distribution challenge. When HMV was in deep trouble, losing money on its production infrastructure to produce records, its focus shifted to create production capacity of the new medium, cassettes. New content creation/acquisition took a back seat, partly because cash was tight.

Fortunately, the new manager recognized the unexploited potential of its core business, content created over time forming an enormous library of music tracks known as 'back catalogue' in the trade, to script its turnaround.

Yes, a turnaround CEO needs to have a 'vision' both to help develop a sustainable strategy and the execution road map. The CEO must decide to stretch himself and the organization to chase a challenging goal—a sustainable revival plan. Unless the CEO challenges himself, circumstances will force him into a daily grind of cost management, that is, cutting costs, which is only a knee-jerk reaction to manage diminishing cash flows, and not, repeat not, a tenable strategy.

Why? Because it begins with decimating a company's operations: closing factories, firing people, selling 'non-core' businesses, and eventually results in a forced exit.

All successful turnarounds are results of positive goals: regain market share, create a viable niche for the company's products and services through innovation, exploit opportunities from unexploited nooks of the core business, create a sustainable business model by extracting value from under-utilized 'assets'.

A canny CEO will, however, keep the grand vision to himself, but will break the goal down into 'doable' short-term objectives and share these objectives with the employees, supported by a well-thought out execution plan.

With each 'small' win, that is, successful execution of a short-term plan, employees will begin to respect the judgement of the

CEO, and will extend full support to the achievement of the next objective, and the next, and be ready to share the grand vision. The HMV story highlights how a 'limited win' can set the ball rolling to eventually win the war.

This is particularly relevant to those companies facing a resource crunch. Most companies requiring a turnaround are cash strapped, unless of course it's Ford, having enough cash in the bank in 2007, despite incurring a seven-billion-dollar loss the previous year!

That's because most under-performing companies would have maxed out on loan facilities, and have a long list of creditors breathing down their necks for overdue payments, before resuming supplies. At times, especially in India, there are other pressing overdue issues, such as defaults on statutory deposits of provident fund, excise duty and sales tax. There may even be some accumulated deferred salary payments.

Even if white knights come in and take over the company, they are rarely willing to bring in more cash than is necessary for a few months working capital.

The turnaround manager will have to be alive to the need to conserve cash and use resources only on productive activities. The more of the new cash is spent on settling old dues, the less will be available for the immediate priority which is to generate an income stream.

Other than keeping the company afloat, the income stream will address a few critical issues: (a) build confidence within the company and its employees, (b) fund some of the activities required for a sustainable revival plan and (c) give confidence to the white knight and/or external lenders to make more money available to implement some of the more expensive initiatives, held back owing to lack of resources.

Perforce the new turnaround manager will be under pressure to look for and maximize the use of under-utilized assets, that is, 'deep mine' all the tangible and intangible assets, including 'legacy' assets, and put these to productive use. No bad thing, as almost all successful turnaround strategies have relied upon 'creative' utilization of assets, either to produce synergistic goods or services or to reach out to new customer segments, or at the very least to generate cash to enable launching of new initiatives.

Broadly, assets can be put into four buckets—fully utilized, under-utilized, neglected or hidden.

The best example of a fully utilized infrastructure asset is probably that of a large business process outsourcing facility with say 3,000 seats. The infrastructure comprising space, work desks, computers, servers, air conditioners, power back up and so on including kitchens, canteens and gyms, are used 24/7.

In contrast, a school infrastructure for 3,000 students is probably utilized for no more than 8 hours. Similarly, there are a number of factories which work 24/6, and others which work only one 8-hour shift six days a week.

Capacity (often a legacy asset) utilization, that is, productivity per machine may also vary from up to 99 per cent rated capacity to an abysmal 50 per cent rated capacity.

Taking a step further, if the same machine is used to produce both high-value and low-value products, then orders permitting, producing only high-value products is a much better utilization of the asset, than producing a mix of high- and low-value products.

If a turnaround manager were to be asked to run a school, he, I have no doubt, would look to monetize free infrastructure time before and after school hours and during holidays and long vacations. Why does this not happen on a routine basis? The answer is because schools are run by educators and not managers. Some US colleges, under pressure to raise financial assistance from private sources, now have a president to manage financial administration, with a dean to focus on maintaining academic excellence.

Botulinum Toxin Type A to Botox

Large companies with a long list of products and services often focus on a few star sellers, while others are allowed to languish in their designated market segment, often as an independent

SBU, with little oversight or support from the top management. Similarly, 'neglected assets' accumulate dust in all companies, especially when two or three star products account for 90 per cent of sales and 95 per cent of profits.

In the 1960s, an ophthalmologist in San Francisco, Alan B. Scott, was researching a condition called strabismus, which makes people cross-eyed. He was interested in Botulinum Toxin Type A, a purified form of the bacterial toxin associated with botulism. When he injected a tiny bit of the substance into cross-eyed monkeys, their pupils realigned. Over the next 20 years, he and another researcher studied the use of the toxin for cross-eyed humans, and, in the late 1970s, Scott formed a company, Oculinum, based on his research.

In due course, Oculinum attracted the attention of Allergan, a big producer of eye-care drugs based in Irvine, California. In 1991, a couple of years after the Food and Drug Administration (FDA) approved the use of Scott's drug for strabismus and other conditions, Allergan bought Oculinum.

Under Allergan's ownership, Botulinum Toxin Type A was sold under the catchier brand name of Botox and attracted a following among ophthalmologists.

Nothing much happened with Botox till David Pyott became the CEO of Allergan in 1998. Worried about stagnating sales and profits at Allergan, David was looking for a platform for growth when he came across some tucked away reports compiling feedback from doctors about an unusual phenomenon arising after the use of Botox: the vertical lines between patients' eyebrows were disappearing after they used Botox!

And what a game changer this turned out to be. Sensing an opportunity, David pushed R&D to aggressively accelerate research on Botox's wrinkle-erasing potential.

In 2002, Allergan gained FDA's approval to market Botox as a product that reduces the appearance of frown lines. In 2001, sales of Botox had barely crossed 200 million dollars; by 2013, sales were nearing two billion dollars and accounted for almost a third of Allergan's revenue.

Postal Services

Postal services in India, the United States and the United Kingdom have been poster boys for reaching out to every nook and corner of their countries and the world for centuries. But the advent of e-mail, e-cards, e-gift vouchers and other digital modes of communication have been ringing the death knells of the post office network since the turn of the century.

Many analysts claim that the vast infrastructure of the postal networks has become a huge 'burden' on tax payers, and the clamour to close down post offices and their services has been gaining ground in all countries with a sizeable postal service network. After all, private players like Western Union can do money transfer more efficiently, UPS and FedEx can deliver parcels faster and of course a click on the computer can send mails in a blink of an eye.

Are all inherited assets, especially 'legacy assets' which by definition have lost usefulness in the present context, useful?

Let me go on a limb and say that, like beauty, the value of any asset lies in the eyes of the beholder. Especially when assets designed for a specific time and purpose, tend to get *hidden under a patina of dust and disrepair* as businesses and business models change.

Are values of these assets too deeply buried to be unlocked?

The India Post Story

One of my childhood heroes has been the intrepid postman, always showing up, come sunshine, rain or hailstorm, on time to deliver post cards, money orders, registered letters and on rare occasions a small parcel.

India has the largest postal network in the world with over 150,000 post offices, dotted all over the country, 90 per cent of which are located in villages. Some of these villages have barely 100 families residing in them. The network has registered a seven-fold growth, in the last 70 years. On an average, a post office serves a population of 8,221 people. India Post employs close to two million people.

But a visit to a post office, in recent times, had become progressively nightmarish. All you saw were decrepit buildings with dark and dingy interiors, hordes of people sitting with no apparent work, on rickety chairs and tables, whiling their time away discussing cricket, the latest Hindi hit movie or some inane political gossip.

Ever since the advent of e-mail and the Internet supported by a rapid expansion of broadband network reaching remote corners of the country and the world, 'snail mail', the often used pejorative term for old-fashioned communication via paper letters, the mainstay of Indian postal services since its inception in 1771, had become virtually extinct.

The post offices also provide other services, *but many pundits continue to opine that the vast post office network is actually a huge financial drain on the country's coffers—the payroll alone of two million employees is mind boggling—and must be dismantled forthwith.*

Fortunately, some customers saw an opportunity to use this network to expand their businesses to hitherto uncharted territories.

Twenty years ago, Shankar, a good friend, was one of the many small entrepreneurs, keen on setting up mail order businesses to reach out to a much wider audience, but lacked the wherewithal to set up a logistics support system similar to the ones set up by the likes of LL Bean and others in the United States.

Shankar was running a music label promoting Carnatic music. He had cassettes produced in Chennai, and wanted to find a cheaper alternative to privately owned courier companies to deliver these cassettes to his customers. Shankar approached his local post office to discuss the possibilities.

Shankar was very pleasantly surprised when two senior post office officers came to visit him, at his office, to discuss the logistics. Unfortunately, no deal was struck as the post office was not confident that his cassettes, packed in cardboard outer cartons would survive the rigours of rough handling at railway stations.

Those were the early days of the Internet. A few e-tailers had made their appearance. They were equally handicapped in reaching their merchandise to remote customers.

Shankar learned from the post office officials that there was a collective realization among the post office management that their legacy assets presented a unique opportunity to develop a sustainable business model, whereby the customers can dramatically increase their market penetration and the post office's revenues can multiply geometrically and help reduce the US$ 1 billion deficit recorded year after year in their financial reports.

All that the post office had to do was upgrade their infrastructure to respond to the needs of this rapidly growing new market segment.

What follows is a brief snapshot of probably the most interesting customer-service provider collaboration in engineering a turn-around of a moribund organization 'burdened with legacy assets' and an army of unproductive workers.

The credit must go to the management of the Indian postal services to wake up to the fact that the vast network under their control can be transformed into a highly profitable money-making machine. They would also thank the likes of Western Union and a bunch of mail order companies and e-tailers for showing them why and how.

Credit must also go the same management for recognizing that the reinvention process would take long, requiring a clear strategy, long-time commitment of resources and patience to see an arduous process bear fruit.

The first challenge was to digitize their operations to speed up transactions, track them and keep customers informed. This required computerization and Internet connectivity at each post office, live uploading of transaction-related data, with bar codes and dedicated banks of servers to keep both the chain of transaction handlers and the customers in the loop. The second challenge was the realization that technology alone will not be enough. A new work culture needed to be created where the employees strive to earn customer satisfaction and happily use technology to be able to do so.

A pilot, Project Arrow, involving 50 post offices in 10 circles, of a quality improvement programme was launched in 2008 to test the sustainability and scalability of an IT-enabled service platform, designed to help each post office become a one stop shop for retail services and a single window facility for banking, money remittances and other financial products and services for social and civic initiatives (Source: India Post Web Site & Newspaper reports).

The programme also aimed to project the post offices as vibrant workplaces equipped with state-of-the-art technology, manned by committed and professionally trained employees. A new name and logo—India Post—was designed to announce the transformation.

Once the infrastructure modernization programme was conceptualized, steering committees and core teams were constituted to flesh out a detailed implementation plan.

Objectives of the Quality Improvement Programme are as follows:

1. Same day mail delivery/transfer to other post offices
2. Signature scanning at savings bank counters to reduce transaction time
3. Web-based immediate remittance services
4. Timely settlement of account-related queries—transfer, closure, deceased claims
5. Continuous tracking and on-time delivery of untampered packages
6. Enhancement in operational and soft skills of staff members
7. Standardization of both exteriors and interiors of post offices

Both quantitative and qualitative measurement norms were set. Performance against key performance indicators (KPIs) were scrutinized through a web-based monitoring mechanism, and shared among various stakeholders through video conferencing. Formation of local citizens' fora and online grievance cells monitored qualitative issues.

Task forces were created with carefully placed 'change agents' and designated leaders to impart training and installation of equipment and software. Steering committees comprising senior managers and the post masters of the participating post offices were responsible for continuous monitoring, adherence to timelines and providing guidance and support at every step.

US$ 700 million was allocated for modernization and digitalization of post offices, and computerization of warehouses to handle higher parcel traffic. Simultaneously, a programme was launched to retrain workers, improve their soft skills while dealing with customers and make them comfortable to work in a computerized environment. The post office website had a new user-friendly look and feel and was designed to respond to most customer queries and requests, ranging from buying stamps to tracking of goods sent to remote corners of the globe.

The programme was ready for a phased national roll out by 2012.

The roll out, constantly monitored against various KPIs, has been successful and, by the end of 2015 almost 30,000 post offices now proudly display the India Post logo, look and feel. *They also delight customers.*

'The postal network and services are the backbone for last-mile connectivity across the country and our efforts at modernization as well as digitization are bearing fruit' telecom and IT minister Ravi Shankar Prasad, who is also in charge of the department of posts, said to *The Times of India*, New Delhi Edition, 4 April 2016.

The numbers support Mr Prasad's claim.

Cash on delivery collections made by India Post for over 800 e-commerce players, including Amazon and Flipkart, is expected to jump by a staggering 360 per cent—US$ 272 million (₹1,800 crores) in 2015–16 (est.) over US$ 75million (₹500 crores) in 2014–15.

Parcel revenue after a decline of 2 per cent in 2013–14 have registered 45 per cent growth in 2014–15 and is expected to exceed 100 per cent year-on-year growth in 2015–16.

Mr Prasad also said, 'With India Post having got a Payments Bank License, there is a scramble to forge partnerships and alliances'.

This is hardly an exaggeration.

While IFC-World Bank is reportedly looking for an equity stake, the number of alliance seekers in various services provided by the post office include among others: Citibank, Deutsche Bank, HSBC, Barclays Bank, State Bank of India, for Banking; HDFC Life, Kotak Life Insurance, ICICI Lombard for insurance and Visa for ATM.

VISION AND MISSION

India Post has now reached a level when they can confidently announce, what the management believes is a *'doable'* vision and mission.

The vision statement is simple and to the point.

India Post's products and services will be the customer's first choice.

It sums up in a few words, the complete change of mindset in the management.

It's a recognition of the new reality: Indian postal services are no longer a monopoly. Customers now have choices. India Post will have to become customer-centric and work hard to become the customer's preferred choice. In many of its operations, it will have to play catch-up.

The mission statements are equally anchored to reality:

- to sustain its position as the largest postal network in the world touching the lives of every citizen in the country;
- to provide mail, parcel, money transfer, banking, insurance and retail services with speed and reliability;
- to provide services to the customers on value-for-money basis;
- to ensure that the employees are proud to be its main strength and serve its customers with a human touch and
- to continue to deliver social security services and to enable last mile connectivity as a Government of India platform.

The mission clearly emphasizes the commitment to maintain the phenomenal reach of its network and offer products and services to the universe it has access to and offer a host of 'value for money', that is, price competitive-products and services with 'speed and reliability'. It recognizes the potential of its human capital to become willing and effective change agents.

It accepts its responsibility 'to deliver social security services' by creating a conduit to every corner of the country on behalf of the Government of India.

THE STRATEGIC GOALS

It is heartening that the post office management has accepted the need to achieve financial self-sufficiency by generating surpluses for services outside 'their universal service obligation', while defining their strategic goals.

- Achieve the long-term goal of financial self-sufficiency by generating surpluses from services (existing and new) outside our universal service obligation.
- Develop, implement and operate a system of standards with accountability for performance.
- Develop a scalable and flexible technology infrastructure to support our operations.
- Be the preferred, trusted and reliable service partner for all customers.
- Ensure that India Post acquires all required people's capabilities to deliver its chosen services portfolio.

Only time will tell how deep and lasting the culture changes will be through this rebranding process.

Let's wish them well in their journey.

Migrating to a New Core Business

Chris Zook, in his article 'Finding Your Next Core Business' first published in April 2007, (reprinted in *HBR* on Strategic Renewal in 2008) says that it's possible to measure the vitality of a company's business core.[1]

His article is based on an in-depth study of 25 companies, some of which were in deep crisis. 'If it (the company) needs reinvention', Zook concludes, 'the best course is to mine hidden assets', having ascertained that in four-fifths of the companies examined, a hidden asset was the centrepiece of the new strategy.

Declining performance in what was a thriving business can often be attributed to execution shortfall. But, Zook argues, if a strategy appears exhausted it's usually for three reasons.

Apple computers was losing market share in a shrinking market, that is, *profit pool*. It got saved by moving its business towards digital music. General Motors lost share to Toyota, because of *inherently inferior economics*, unable as it was to readily shake off legacy structures and costs.

The third reason is when a company finds out that *its growth formula cannot be sustained*. Nokia is a recent example of a market leader in cell phones stalling because nimble-footed competitors were easily replicating its once unique source of differentiation.

Managements react differently when they discover that a core business is under pressure. Apple used its design and technology capabilities to find another core business with the iPod. General Motors took a long time to respond to the Toyota threat, and has not been able to regain its pre-Japanese car market shares. Nokia management exited the cell phone handset making business and sold it to Microsoft. Nokia has used the proceeds to strengthen other core businesses.

Companies deep mining assets have found, more often than not, that a pleasant surprise awaits.

The Botox phenomenon underline Chris Zook's observation 'the history of corporate transformation shows you're more likely to be successful if you seek change in your own backyard' and adds that these backyards, can hide potential winners in 'undervalued business platforms'. These could be undeveloped adjacencies, non-core businesses and/or orphan products.

---

[1] Zook, Chris. 2007. 'Finding Your Next Core Business', Harvard Business Review, 85 (4).

Botox, a non-core business for Allergan, was very close to being relegated to an orphan, before its true potential was discovered.

From Absorption Refrigeration to RV Interior Systems

The second gem hidden in the backyard often is 'untapped insight into customer's minds and needs' uncovered by careful analysis into unrecognized segments of the market, privileged access to and trust among the company's loyal users and under-utilized data and information. Mr Zook illustrates this through a case study of Dometic.

'Dometic's roots go back to 1922 when two students acquired a patent when they applied absorption technology to refrigeration. Unlike household refrigerators which use compressors driven by electrical motors, the Dometic fridge required only a source of heat such as a propane tank to do the job, and was particularly useful for small boats and RVs, recreational vehicles.

Electrolux acquired the patent rights in 1925 and Dometic continued to work as an independent division, chugging along with revenues under US$ 20 million, but with diminishing profits. By the early 1970s, it began losing money.

A new CEO, Stork, took over and began the search for new customers.

He moved aggressively into hotel minibars, where the absorption technology's silent operation was a real plus. The company's sales and profits began to look up.

The real breakthrough came when Stork's team focused on gaining more insight into RV owner needs. Dometic was not looking to sell more refrigerators to this group, they already had monopoly. They were looking to sell other products using their customer database and existing relationships. Soon they were able to add air-conditioning, automated awnings, generators, systems for cooking, lighting, water purification and sanitation to the Dometic line'.[2]

---

[2] Zook, Chris. 2007. 'Finding Your Next Core Business', Harvard Business Review, 85 (4).

In the process, Dometic's core business shifted to becoming a highly profitable one stop shop for all RV systems, and it emerged as a major channel for trade for these goods, which further added to the bottom line.

The third asset often hidden in the backyard is 'capabilities'— untapped corporate capabilities, non-core capabilities in different divisions and of course underleveraged core capabilities in different divisions.

From Optical Storage Devices to LED Lighting

Moser Baer India Limited, headquartered in New Delhi, is a leading global tech-manufacturing company. Established in 1983, the company is one of the world's largest manufacturers of optical storage media such as CDs and DVDs.

Every fifth disc manufactured globally belongs to Moser Baer and it is the lowest cost optical media manufacturer in the world. The company is also the first to market next-generation of storage formats such as Blu-ray discs and HD-DVD in India.

Over the years, the company has entered into exciting areas of solid-state media with the launch of pen drives and flash memory cards, content replication, home entertainment and is a market leader in the high growth photovoltaic (PV) space.

The company has a presence in over 100 countries, serviced through 15 marketing offices and representatives in India, the United States, Europe, Japan, Russia, Ukraine, Egypt, Argentina, Chile, Malaysia and has strong tie-ups with many global technology players in the optical media storage business. In the PV space, the company has a presence in the entire value chain with products being sold to more than 82 countries.

Its products are manufactured at its three state-of-the-art manufacturing facilities located in the suburbs of New Delhi employing over 8,000 employees. Through its wholly owned subsidiaries, the company manufactures PV cells and modules using crystalline silicon and thin film technologies.

The last few years have been difficult for the company owing to rapid changes in the optical storage device market. The year 2014 was a particularly challenging year sustained through business portfolio rationalization and transition of technology. Operations have been restructured keeping undiluted focus on the company's core competencies in the storage media market, while building on strengths in emerging businesses for sustainable growth.

A recent focus area is solid-state lighting (SSL). A pilot phase, targeting mainly the professional segment is now in the process of being ramped up as a full-fledged business.

The company believes that it is in a position to tap this opportunity in India on account of its strong brand equity and key capabilities:

- precision-molding assets and capabilities (from the optical media business),
- surface mount technology assets and capabilities (from the SSL business),
- relevant experience and know-how related to product quality and reliability, design, product development, testing and optics,
- global sourcing strengths and
- strengths in indian sales, marketing and distribution which can be synergistically exploited.

Source: Moser Baer 2014–15 Annual Report.

Given Moser Baer's earlier track record in successfully dealing with many disruptions in their core businesses, there is no reason to believe that their most recent transformation will not succeed, especially as the strategy builds on known strengths.

CHAPTER 8

OPPORTUNITY KNOCKS ONLY ONCE
SUB-OPTIMAL UTILIZATION OF ASSETS

Every company over time creates some assets. Some are tangible. Some are intangible. Some are a combination of the two. Some are created. Some are acquired.

Many are neglected. Many are forgotten. Many are sold for a pittance. Many remain buried.

What is the best place for a company to bury its assets? Believe it or not, it's the balance sheet.

Many is the time one reads about dramatic changes in the fortunes of an under-performing company after a merger or after being taken over by a new management.

ArcelorMittal

The beginning of the ArcelorMittal conglomerate can be traced back to the time when LN Mittal set up his first steel plant in Indonesia, in 1976. Reportedly, his success thereafter has largely been built on buying up loss-making state-owned mills and quickly turning them around.

Mr Mittal had one of his most notable successes in late 1989, when he turned around a loss-making government-funded steel firm in Trinidad and Tobago which was losing US$ 1 million a day. Within a year, Mr Mittal's turnaround team was able to double the output, halve the operations cost and make the business profitable.

Mr Mittal followed the same strategy in former Soviet republic of Kazakhstan, and took over the state-owned blast furnace steel plant in 1995. His turnaround team was again able to double production, find a new market in China for its products and make the company profitable within a year. In between he had acquired stressed steel plants in Mexico, Canada, Germany and Ireland.

The crowning glory came in 2006, when Mr Mittal took over European steel giant Arcelor SA for US$ 33 billion. The merged entity, renamed ArcelorMittal, with the Mittal family owning controlling shares of the combined group, became the world's largest steel producer.

The success of the Mittal group is often attributed to his turnaround team who had honed their skills in spotting hidden assets in the balance sheet, notably under-utilized capacity, and finding solutions to quickly optimize production and eliminate wasteful expenses.

A similar story is unfolding, as I write this in the United Kingdom.

Liberty House, a metal-trading company set up by Sanjeev Gupta during his student days in college, is in the news as a potential buyer of some of the Tata Corus steel plants in the United Kingdom.

Over the last decade and a half, Mr Gupta has grown Liberty House into a business with a £4.2 billion turnover, with its activities ranging from steel-making to renewable energy, financial services and property.

Liberty House is best known in Wales for buying the former Alpha Steel works in Newport in 2013, and reopening production there in the autumn of 2015 as other steel plants around the country were closing down or being sold.

More recently, at the end of April 2016, Mr Gupta completed acquisition of two loss-making rolling mills at Clyde Bridge and Dalzell in Scotland from the Tata Group. He is now evaluating a bid for other troubled assets of the Tata Group in the United Kingdom, including the one at Port Talbot.

The problem with Port Talbot, from Mr Gupta's point of view, is its size and the fact it is built around blast furnaces making liquid steel from ores. The model that Liberty House is building at Newport and elsewhere is built around melting down scrap metal—two million tons a year at Newport—using modern electric arc furnaces.

'Why make primary steel in a blast furnace when you already have secondary steel (in the form of scrap)? Why don't we *recycle* the scrap first?' He asked in a recent interview.

It's an interesting perspective, why create more scrap when you can recycle a portion of the mountain of scrap lying around? Would the British government, keen to prevent job losses if the Port Talbot plant is closed, help Mr Gupta access the sizeable funds required to purchase the new furnaces to switch to making steel from scrap?

Typically, a company balance sheet will itemize physical assets as fixed assets, but rarely mention 'assets' created over time, unless monetized, as assets. This is strange, because in today's world these are the assets which give the company critical edges over competitors, and provide the platform for long-term growth and profitability.

Today's businesses pivot around IP to hold on to market share, provide breakthroughs into new market segments and build barriers to competitors entries.

For example, a pharmaceutical company's 'assets' column in the balance sheet will certainly include the cost of putting up the state-of-the-art R&D labs and manufacturing facilities. These may have cost a pile, but contribute little to its perceived 'valuation'.

Why? Because the market cap of the company will be driven solely by the investor expectation of the sales and profits owing to (a) the number of years of exclusivity remaining on its existing 'formulation' patents, (b) the list of 'applied for' patents in the pipeline and (c) the number of applications pending with FDA seeking clearance to market new formulations.

These may be mentioned in the director's report, but will rarely feature in the assets column in the balance sheet.

Similarly, Disney's valuation will be based on the copyrights it has on its creations and acquisitions—movies, music, theatrical productions, toys, books and so on. The physical assets Disney has—studios, theme parks and such—will be a part, but a very small part of the valuation, but will feature prominently in the assets column in its balance sheet.

Apple's phenomenal brand equity and the resultant market cap was built upon its research, design and marketing capabilities—unlikely to be reflected in the assets column of its balance sheet and has little to do with its physical assets, the value of which must be relatively small as Apple's manufacturing is largely outsourced.

Assets created over time are soft skills and capabilities—not recorded in balance sheets—but can be game changers. Using them can make companies. Ignoring them can break companies.

A discussion on some of the ignored opportunities to migrate to new businesses using existing assets, may help in appreciating asset utilization strategies better.

A Lost Opportunity?

We read about the exit of HM from the Indian automobile market in Chapter 4. Many market analysts would have forecast the demise of HM, as soon as the Indian market opened up in the 1990s, and all global auto majors came in with large investments to tap the untapped potential.

True, Maruti not only survived in this scenario, but also thrived. That's because its Japanese partner had the necessary funds to bring in new car platforms and upgrade their cars to conform to rapidly changing fuel efficiency, permissible emission and safety norms.

I am assuming that the HM promoters either did not have the funds to make the additional investments required to tool up to retain its position in the market, or did not want to because of the uncertainties on how the market will shape up with so many top players in the arena.

Looking only at HM's balance sheet assets—'obsolete' component manufacturing and car assembly plants, and a paint shop in Uttarpara, a suburb of Kolkata—exiting the car market was probably the right decision. But even this obsolete plant combined *with its unreported (and unappreciated) assets*—a trained workforce, an extensive pan-India dealer network and a spider web of repair garages dotted across the country—could have been the platform to build a new business.

Since the automobile market in India was so small till the mid–1990s with barely a quarter million cars coming into the market, that too after Maruti's entry, car owners continued to use a car till it died, literally. New cars were not readily available. It was worth waiting a few more months to see what the global majors were bringing in.

That apart there was no reliable used car market to unload your car and buy another 'second-hand car' to tide you over till you could buy a Chevy, a Fiat, a Cielo, a Hyundai or a Honda, shortly.

The second-hand car market, as it existed then, was chaotic. There were quite a few 'independent' dealers, with lots, occupied by some tired-looking Ambys, premiers, a Tata Sierra or the odd-tattered imported cars. The dealers or their sales assistants looked ready to scalp inexperienced first-time car buyers, pointing to obviously doctored milometres showing much fewer miles on them, than the body betrayed, and claiming that the retreaded tyres were actually new. There were no insurance papers, and no guarantees. Once you drove out of the lot, the car was yours, and those undisclosed faults you could not find were your crosses to bear.

Imagine the opportunity a reputed car manufacturer with their extensive dealer and repair shop network had, to change the look and feel of this market—showrooms displaying polished exteriors and interiors of diligently refurbished cars which looked as good as new, manned by well-mannered, friendly car salesmen and women, offering a six month guarantee and *certified by HM*, no less.

There were neighbouring markets as well to tap. Import duties on new cars were so high in Sri Lanka, Bangladesh and Nepal, that only refurbished cars could be imported. An opportunity left for exploitation by Maruti and Mahindra when they launched their pre-owned cars later. And if *Business Standard* (November 2014) got it right, the used car market in India is not only growing faster than new cars, it is actually bigger than the new car market size.

> The used-car business is 1.3 times bigger than the new-car market and growing at a faster rate, says former Maruti Suzuki managing director Jagdish Khattar, who now runs a multi-brand car services company Carnation Auto. According to rough estimates, almost three million second-hand cars were sold in India last year compared to the 2.5 million new cars.

I submit that a turnaround manager would have looked at HM's residual physical assets and its core business experience and competencies of HM, as assets which could have been used to kick start a credible *pre-owned car business* in India.

A Positioning Fiasco?

Tata Nano sold 21,000 units in 2015–16, a shade less than 10 per cent of their production capacity of 250,000 per annum and a lot less, I am sure, than what Tata would have forecast as sales, seven years after its much lauded and publicized launch in 2009.

Nano was unveiled to the world in early January 2008 at the Delhi Auto Expo. It became a media darling overnight with *Time* magazine writing 'it could well be one of the most important cars ever designed...' to *Newsweek* claiming Nano to be 'a new breed of 21st century cars' to *The Financial Times* stating that the Nano, the tiny car with an even tinier price tag, could well be the symbol of India's claim to be a modern nation (Chacko, Noronha and Agrawal 2010).[1]

---

[1] Chacko, Philip, Christabelle Noronha, and Sujata Agrawal. 2010. Small Wonder: The Making of the Nano. Westland Ltd., Copyright Tatasons.

Media from other countries and at home, India, were equally enthralled. Comparisons with Ford Model T were frequently made.

Potential buyers were equally enthralled. More than 200,000 advance booking of the car reflected the customer excitement.

The numbers forecast for the demand of Nano by experts were so large that many environmentalists began worrying about the emission effect when Nano reaches its sales potential. Competitors like Maruti even contemplated reducing the prices of their entry level 800 model.

Nano is a brilliant example of a company using its non-balance sheet assets to make a 'world beater'. Tata used its design and engineering skills and of course its deep pockets to develop the car. It also used its corporate goodwill to generate enough free press and TV time to make Nano a household name overnight. A dealer network was ready too.

Soon after the announcement of Nano's launch, a new plant was set up to produce the Nano. This plant is now lying with 90 per cent capacity unutilized.

What has gone wrong? The answer is marketing, or rather the absence of marketing.

Effective marketing is always one of the key success factors in consumer product sales. Marketing was not a well-honed skill in Tata Motors' formidable assets armoury, but was available, I presume, in other group companies, notably Taj Hotels.

Early hiccups faced in setting up its production plant—a mid-course setback requiring the shift of its plant from Bengal to Gujarat—meant that Tata would take almost 18 months to clear the delivery backlog from the pre-orders, which seemed to have lulled the company into a sense of complacency. There was no visible effort to build a brand and reach out to a target audience with a clear positioning.

It allowed the media to create its 'positioning'. And by default its unique selling proposition became 'the world's cheapest car'.

True, India is a price-conscious market. Indian consumers love to bargain. But does that mean they want to be seen driving the cheapest car? The answer is obviously 'no'. Especially among those who are in income brackets thinking of buying a car, a prestige symbol.

No consumer product company, and a car company is one, would ever allow a product to be launched unless it has decided which segment to address and how to competitively position the product in that segment.

Markets do have segments for the conscious price, and companies do cater to those segments but take care to position their products as 'better value for money' appealing to those who believe they are canny buyers and do not want to be taken for a ride. They will never sell their product as 'cheap', and certainly not as 'the cheapest in the world' which has very different connotations from saying the 'best value for money'.

Tata Motors was guilty of confusing media's excitement about the cheapest car with consumer perception of the buyer of the 'cheapest' car.

They erred in not proactively positioning the Nano as desirable to, say, the 18 to 20 year olds (or their doting grand dads) talking about its design, ease in manoeuvring in busy city streets, fuel efficiency, lower emissions and of course the 'oomph' factor in having your own car to drive on your first day to college or the safety in driving your own car back in the evening as opposed to facing harassment in public buses and trains.

The Nano colours suggested that Tata had a young target customer in mind, perhaps a little older than the first year college girl, probably one of the many thousands working in IT companies. If only, they had the gumption to reserve pre-launch bookings for this target audience, Nano would certainly not have ended up as *another lost opportunity*.

The paradox is that within the Tata group, there is a hotel division, which has mastered the art of positioning different products for different target segments, with properties ranging from the ultra-luxury Lake Palace Hotel, Udaipur to the value for money Ginger Hotels. I doubt whether the Tata Motors management ever consulted the Taj Hotels marketing team.

Why do existing managements fail to spot these hidden assets, when most turnaround managers not only find them, but use them to save so many companies?

Being too close to the daily grind might explain the myopia of the present management. We have looked at some of the causes of failure in earlier chapters. Invariably, the problems are results of tunnel vision and the absence of an entrepreneurial approach to problem solving. Entrepreneurs know no boundaries, and have little fear of the uncharted path. They have no holy cows, neither do they believe in sacred and inviolable legacies, rites and rituals. Entrepreneurs do not dream, they see opportunities; they do not see liabilities, they see under-utilized assets.

Perhaps this is why so many private equity (PE) investment funds are keen on buying a stake in under-performing companies, and turning them around.

Partners in PE firms are by definition entrepreneurs and risk takers by inclination. When they evaluate a company, they look at assets—remember the beauty (and therefore the value) of assets lie in the eyes of the beholder—and see *how these can be exploited and not how they are currently exploited.*

PE firm partners understand people as assets better. They know that money can buy any plant and machinery and the building to house them, but these investments alone will not make money, especially if they are legacy assets of loss-making companies, probably idling for most of the time or neglected.

But people and people skills are forever. PE partners want to know the people who will run the organization when the PE support comes in. They want to gauge the levels of commitment to the organization, the energy levels and the aspirations of the people available to support the new CEO because PE firms also know that only a new CEO can pull the distressed company out of the woods.

PE firms are now busy structuring asset reconstruction companies (ARCs) but have realized that unless there is an asset management company to work in tandem, they may not be able to get maximum buck for their investment. Otherwise they will go the 'vulture fund' way-strip physical assets and sell them piecemeal, and hope to make a little money. A tall order at the best of times!

Even Mr LN Mittal had a turnaround team in place before he went on a buying spree. There is no shame in learning from a Guru.

Creativity at Its Best

Bed and breakfast (B&B) as a concept is not new by any stretch of imagination. They must have been around since the days of the early travellers, when the taverns were full, and weary pilgrims would be taken in by villagers for the night, probably for a small consideration.

Over the years, B&Bs became viable alternatives to inns and hotels for budget travellers, especially in places a little distance away from big cities.

If you were a low-budget world traveller in say the year 2004, you would have certainly picked up a copy of Lonely Planet and look for a place to stay in from the listings of B&Bs and pensioners from big cities to small villages in England, France and Italy.

For some strange reason, B&Bs never became visible or popular in the United States and the rest of America, Eastern Europe and most of Asia.

In a new city, a first-time traveller may find it a little difficult to choose a location and a room not having any references about safety, hygiene, friendliness of the 'hosts' or the quality of breakfast on offer, especially in cities where language is a barrier.

In the pre-internet days, you had to buy 'blind'; but today you can read postings and blogs and ratings given by a wide variety of travellers.

Asset utilization at a micro-level at its best: an empty bed at night is an under-utilized asset. Fried eggs and toast in the morning add value. Putting the bed to use eases the burden on the housewife to have to stretch her budget at all times; win–win transaction for all.

A couple of entrepreneurs see the opportunity to link them—the asset owner and the potential overnight 'guest'—together, and create a user-friendly web booking site for hosts to register and guests to book stays. Where do they launch the site? Obviously, the United States, with a gaping hole in this segment.

The site is launched in 2008.

In March 2009, the name Airbedandbreakfast.com was shortened to Airbnb.com, and the site's content had expanded from air beds and shared spaces to a variety of properties including entire homes and apartments, private rooms, castles, boats, manors, tree houses, tipis, igloos, private islands and other properties.

It was the summer of 1998 in Lima, Peru.

Our hired car had left for the night, when Preeti, my wife, and I had the urge to go out to eat an American-style burger. I remember seeing a McDonald's earlier in the day, but a little distance away from our small hotel.

How do we get there? Public transport in Lima was chaotic. Metred taxis were rare. No Bahas (Bajaj auto-rickshaws) in sight.

I suddenly spot a small car parked on the side with a cardboard placard, a handwritten TAXI sign on it, prominently displayed on the windshield.

The gentleman sitting on the driver's seat turned out to be a government employee who owned his own car, and used to ply it as a taxi after office hours, to make a much needed extra buck. Apparently, the Lima municipality, acutely aware of the inadequacy of the city's transport system encouraged car owners to use their cars whenever they had the time.

Obviously, there was no metre. Fortunately, we discovered that this particular car driver was fluent in English. He explained that the custom was to agree on a fare with the passenger beforehand and then proceed to the destination. He also explained that he was free to pick up one more passenger, going in the same direction. But, out of kindness to us, tourists who have come all the way from India, he said he will not do so on this trip.

He also said that he knew many others who owned cars to be on the roads to ferry passengers in the evening. It was better than sitting at home watching TV, or get bored doing household chores.

I asked whether there were many running such 'taxis' full time. If you wanted to do that, he said, you had to acquire a taxi license, and by law, be on the road to pick up passengers for 12 hours a day. Not many wanted to do that.

There it was for all to see—a huge inventory of available car hours, and willing drivers, looking to make an extra buck. Not just in Lima, Peru, but everywhere else, especially in cities where driving can be a chore and parking a bigger and expensive chore and where DUI penalties are stiff.

An opportunity knocked. Someone had to find a way to connect the dots and then cross the tees to get car owners, drivers, fares and a payment gateway together and develop a mobile app to make it simple, hassle free.

Two friends, Travis Kalanick and Garrett Camp, did just that and Uber was born.

CHAPTER 9

WHO LEADS THE WAY?
THE PROFILE OF A TURNAROUND CEO

The Environment

Successful turnarounds across geographies and industries ranging from retail, hospitality, automobiles, chemicals, computers and business machines, to steel, textile and mobile phones, almost always make strategic moves towards diversification into new product portfolios and allied businesses.

Adoption of new product and process strategies, in a once successful company, is the biggest challenge facing the present management.

In stable companies, the line managers get used to performing their tasks routinely, because experience has taught them that today's tasks are unlikely to be different from yesterday's or for that matter tomorrow's. Their aim is to ensure orderly running of the machine, which is best achieved if 'distractions' are ignored.

Some of the 'distractions' the operating managers may be 'too busy to deal with' may well be, and often are, emerging trends which may over time, significantly impact the business environment in which the company operates.

Reading and paying adequate attention to emerging trends, while doing a demanding job, are never easy, especially as some trends turn out to be mere fads, and will have no lasting impact. The more visible and in-your-face changes often turn out to be such transient fads. Examples abound in the fashion industry, be it in clothes, shoes or other accessories.

Trends in technology development, on the other hand, can fast forward into rapid disruptions of markets, as witnessed in the digital world, be it with iPads, mobiles or Skype.

The subtle changes are the most difficult to sense and interpret in the context of one's business. These gather momentums slowly and often appear to be too far from the core business of the company for the management to 'waste time on'. A good example is that of mobile phones leapfrogging pagers in many 'emerging' markets, leading to premature deaths of lithium battery manufacturing companies whose business model centred on capacity building to cater to an anticipated long run of pagers before making way for mobiles.

Changes in the demographic profile and consequent lifestyle changes can dramatically change the business environment, but happen far too slowly to raise regular red flags, and leave many an apparently well-run company wondering what hit them when the change acquires critical mass, as it must, when a new generation becomes the major decision-maker.

Heightened awareness of the environment degradation, for example, a live issue among the younger generation, till recently shrugged off as yet another fad, can create ripples which lead to closure of thermal and nuclear power plants at one end of the spectrum, and boycotting a certain brand of jeans at the other end of the same spectrum.

A well-managed company anticipates external environmental changes and modifies their business model to remain in sync with the new reality, thus ensuring a continuing stable environment for the company, much like McDonald's, the poster boy in fast foods, introducing salads as sides in their 'mini meals' as an alternative to the ever-popular high cholesterol French fries!

Under-achieving companies, on the other hand, remain far too focused on their own routine, to notice environmental changes on time. The managers of such companies are destined to be rudely awakened by the monster called sudden discontinuity sooner rather than later.

When the wake-up call happens, the present management is not ready to deal with the needs of the hour—redefine the business, identify areas of new demand and realign the company's capabilities to respond to the challenges of the new operational environment.

Such transformation demands drastic changes in the company's thinking process and its approach to problem solving. The task for the top management is not only to define the new mission and develop an operating strategy, but also to carry the rest of the company to believe in the mission, and wholeheartedly participate in the implementation of the strategy. Legislating a change in the work content and style is never enough. Someone has to provide the leadership that will change the mindset of the employees to adapt to the demands of the new environment and perform to the best of their ability.

Empirical evidence suggests that the incumbent management is rarely, if ever, capable of donning the mantle of effective change agents, boxed in as they have been in traditional operating styles and paralyzed into inactivity as discontinuity in the traditional business gathers momentum.

A new change agent is required to orchestrate the transformation and that too at the very top. Not surprisingly, therefore, almost all successful turnarounds are led by new CEO inducted as the change agents.

Who inducts the new CEO, and how? This depends on the structure of the company.

Closely Held Companies

In India, as in many other countries, a large number of underachieving companies are still managed by the original promoters or their children and grandchildren, who continue to hold controlling shares in the company. Typically, the board comprises other family members or trusted friends, some of whom occupy executive positions and those who do not, fill the quota of non-executive 'independent directors' to comply with company law stipulations. By definition, such companies have large 'doubtful' debts and have to suffer bank or financial institution nominees on the board. Such nominee board members rarely have the seniority to stand up to the family scions who are invariably well connected. As a result, such boards are often toothless.

The decision to induct a new CEO in such set ups is not easy. No matter how enlightened the family members are, letting go on day-to-day controls is perceived as an admission of weakness. The temptation often is to find a new CEO but keep him at the end of short puppet strings.

An Indian Owner Managed Business Group

Note: All * positions are normally reserved for family members.

When faced with a turnaround challenge, it is imperative that the owner defines his own role. Clearly he is an investor, with a significant shareholding, and will continue to be one. When the company has been under-performing or has become distressed under the existing management hierarchical structure, he needs to accept that he or his family members have failed at the task, and a new CEO must not only be inducted, but also given the authority to act.

The Shareholders Responsibility

Analyses of under-performing companies reveal that almost always the losses are funded by lenders and creditors. Everyday cash requirements are met, if at all, by defaulting on payment of interest, and reneging on principal repayment. The lenders know that soon they will be asked to write-off interest dues and convert the principals into zero interest debentures or equity. They also know that they will be called upon to infuse more funds to turn the company around.

The financiers, banks and financial institutes, have a responsibility to their investors. It is their duty to protect such investments. That is why they ask for and get representation on the boards of companies they lend money to in doling out largesse or writing-off investments they are guilty of abusing this trust. They are therefore beholden to the task of persuading the owner that he has abdicated all rights to managing the company, once the company is heading towards distress. The management of the company has to be entrusted to a new CEO. And the new CEO must be allowed to be his own man.

Unfortunately, even in instances where financiers have insisted on induction of new management, the owner has often been entrusted with the task of finding the new CEO. As a result, cronyism has continued with a cosmetic change of faces.

The board, especially, the directors appointed by the lenders must be given the authority to select the new CEO. The owner has to be persuaded to set up a selection committee for this task, and neither the owner, nor any of his family members should be a part of this committee.

Such cronyism is often found in government-owned public sector units as well, the difference being that bureaucrats tend to behave like owners. To make matters worse, the bureaucrats are subject to political pressures as well. That apart they are able to exert undue influence on institutional lenders in India, for example, where nationalized banks have a large share of corporate banking, and prevail on them to continue funding distressed units often to please their political masters. Nothing short of privatization is likely to change this scenario.

The Chief Operating Officer Option

Many companies resort to appointing a COO to take over the day-to-day running of the business, allowing the CEO to remain the public face.

If the downhill trend is detected early enough, and if the business is high profile and people centric, this is often a good move. In the late 1980s, EMI Music realized that they needed to aggressively expand its repertoire and artist's roster to maintain its position as a leading global music company. A COO, with experience in mergers and acquisitions, was brought in, who concentrated on the acquisition of other major labels. The COO then proceeded to restructure EMI's organization and operations, using the larger management pool available to him after the mergers.

The incumbent CEO, who was a well-known and respected industry veteran, stayed on for some time. He represented continuity to EMI's earlier contracted artists, who are known to be temperamental, and needed handling by the people they had dealt with in the past. His presence also reduced the nervousness among some of the long-term company employees, especially those in creative roles, as they, like the artists, were temperamental and identified more readily with the person at the top, rather than the company. That apart, the CEO continued to represent the company in the industry association, which was very active at the time as new technologies (digital) were emerging and new markets (China and East Europe) were opening up. The CEO's experience and personal equation with other industry chiefs came in handy at a difficult time, and free from the responsibilities of running EMI, he was able to devote adequate time in protecting the industries' interest in negotiations with hardware manufacturers as well as new governments legislating anti-piracy regimes.

In this case, the induction of the COO worked out very well, largely because of the nature of the business, which permitted a scenario where the COO could be left alone to do his job, as the CEO had a meaningful role to play outside every day running of the company.

American corporations are prone to appoint COOs as understudies to CEOs, as it is an accepted succession planning tool. In instances where the COO spends too long in the wings, waiting for the CEO to move out, he is often too closely identified with the current culture of the company to be an effective change agent when the need arises. That apart it creates confusion in the decision-making hierarchy, and all important matters end up being referred to the CEO.

In distressed companies, a COO option will not work.

The CEO is unlikely to own up to his responsibility for the present plight of the company and consequently, will not bring a COO on board on his own accord. The board will have to thrust a COO on him, and it is a reasonable assumption that in such circumstances the CEO will not allow the COO any room to manoeuvre. More importantly, an important precondition to the turnaround effort—requirement of a new change agent at the top—will not be met.

Other textbook options, such as empowering managers down the line are unlikely to work for the same reasons. The CEO is unlikely to be a party to the empowering process, especially if outside forces such as banks and financial institutes' nominee directors demand such distribution of authority.

Clearly, therefore, the turnaround process in a sick company must start with the appointment of a competent new CEO, appointed by an effective board and not by the owners and other vested interests.

CEO SELECTION

Rarely, if ever, would there be promotable talent within a distressed company. High quality second line managers, having read the writing on the wall early, would have moved to safer havens. Among those who have stayed behind, there would be a fair amount of jockeying for power, especially as the CEO's stature diminishes.

Promoting any one from this lot is stoking a highly avoidable fire. The reasons are many.

To begin with, each one of them would be comfortable in the existing company culture, which would have developed a high level of tolerance for slackness and inefficiencies, inevitable in a company on a downward spiral. That apart, most of these managers would be more comfortable making incremental improvements than making dramatic changes.

And finally, none of them would be able to command respect and loyalty from those passed over for the top job.

The best bet, and probably the only option is to recruit from outside.

The Turnaround CEO Profile

Job descriptions for general managers, especially CEOs, are always difficult to write, as these positions require operational flexibility.

Delineation of the task in turning a company around is that much more difficult, especially if the brief is to remain in the same business and work with limited resources.

In general terms, the CEO will be expected to bring in a clear vision with a blueprint for a redesigned architecture and provide strong leadership to implement an integrated plan for crisis survival and post-crisis success. Ergo, the new CEO will have to be well equipped with entrepreneurial flair and skills—specifically, an instinct for risk-taking, sure decision-making, comfort in a leadership role and confidence in difficulty—to be able to orchestrate and mastermind dramatic changes when required.

H. Igor Ansoff, in his book *Corporate Strategy*, describes the difference between the operating styles of companies which are stable and those which are not.

Stable companies, dealing at best with incremental changes, need a competitive operating style. Under-achieving or unstable companies, facing discontinuity, require an entrepreneurial style.

Styles	Stable Company	Distressed Company
Attribute	Competitive	Entrepreneurial
Occurrence	Serial and continual	Random and episodic
Direction of change	Continuation of past	Discontinuity
Size of change	Small	Large
Relevance of traditional capabilities	High	Low
Problem familiarity	Related experience	Novel

Source: Ansoff (1970).[1]

Clearly, therefore, the turnaround CEO will have to have an entrepreneurial flair and hence a search among those who have demonstrated such flair is most likely to find a suitable candidate.

Managers heading a venture management group or a new product development division in well-managed multi-product, multi-country companies are good potential candidates. Such people would have demonstrated their entrepreneurial flair and innovativeness—the key qualities necessary in a turnaround manager. That apart, they would have lived with budgetary disciplines and small support structures. They would be mentally tough too, having experienced and overcome disappointments in the market place which has always been good training for a turnaround job.

Importantly, such managers will be the ones who read management articles, attend seminars and workshops and remain aware of developments in diverse businesses and industries. They are also digitally literate, knowing how to use digital tools to plan and monitor projects, and reach out to channels and customers, an essential skill in today's business environment.

An important factor is that they would have worked differently from the run-of-the-mill operating managers, who tend to specialize in certain disciplines. In developing new products or spearheading new ventures, such managers would have interacted and

---

[1] Ansoff, Igor. 1970. Corporate Strategy. London: Penguin Books.

often guided diverse functions such as R&D, production, logistics, sales and distribution, product management, advertising and promotions and pricing. More importantly, they would have learnt how to get work done by peers, as such managers rarely have large departments with direct reports with specific domain expertise.

Leadership Qualities

There are no magic formulae for turnarounds. It will take time, be a hard grind.

The new CEO must be mentally tough, with the stamina and will to battle it out. He must also have self-belief, bordering on arrogance, because he will often be alone, in the early days, in believing that a turnaround is possible especially as precious moments of small successes will not come soon.

There are chapters and verses written on leadership attributes, largely based on character analysis of successful business leaders.

I find a leadership guide developed by FedEx, an excellent reference manual to evaluate the leadership qualities required in a potential turnaround CEO.

1. *Charisma: This is by far the most difficult attribute to assess. FedEx defines it as the person's ability to make others proud to be associated with him. He is a person who is able to make everyone around enthusiastic about assignments and is able to transmit a sense of mission to the subordinates.*

2. *Concern for the individual: This is particularly relevant when dealing with the shaky managers in an under-achieving company. Typically, a good leader is known to coach, advise and teach. He treats each subordinate individually and as individuals. He values each worker and has respect for his contribution, however small. He is able to delegate but does not abdicate, thus creating anxiety and uncertainty. He is prepared to listen and makes time to provide feedback.*

3. *Intellectual ability: He is able to create an environment, which seeks reason and evidence. He asks 'why?' and encourages others to do so. He is not only able to provide new ideas but also able to make his subordinates think in new ways.*

4. *Courage: He has the courage of conviction and the tenacity to persist against all odds. Above all, he has the courage to carry the 'can', 'if' and 'when', when something goes wrong. He is not in the business of finding scapegoats.*
5. *Dependable: He is consistent and honours his commitments. He is also accessible and available.*
6. *Integrity: He believes in a code of ethics and is prepared to fight for principles. To him, the company's interest is always supreme. He does not abuse management privileges.*
7. *Judgement: His judgement is based on facts, reasoning and logic. Whenever he takes a decision on gut feeling, he is able to explain why he is backing his instincts, normally with empirical evidence.*
8. *Self-motivated: He has a high degree of self-motivation and a sense of purpose.*
9. *Energy: He has very high levels of energy, both physical and mental, and brings an infectious enthusiasm for the task on hand.*

The million-dollar question is how to evaluate these qualities in a person in an interview or a series of interviews. I am afraid I have no answer. Perhaps the board should nominate someone who is conversant with interview techniques to specifically probe these qualities and agree to abide by the nominee's selection, or depend on general references and infer whether the candidate has displayed these attributes in his/her previous jobs.

The Discipline Domain Expertise

If it is not possible to entice the CEO, with the right attributes, of another company to join the under-performing company, the search has to focus on the next level of managers, those who are heading departments in other companies—finance, manufacturing, marketing, human resource development (HRD), supply chain, logistics and operations. Few companies have separate strategic planning, new product development or venture management as independent departments, as managers heading these functions are likely to report to one of the functional departments.

The choice more often than not narrows down to two disciplines: marketing and finance.

Given the importance of culture transformation, morale boosting, extensive training and retraining and promoting cross-functional team orientation to resolve issues, HRD is increasingly seen as a discipline which throws up potential CEOs. The turn-around CEO certainly needs a competent HR manager on his turnaround team, but I am not sure whether an HR manager will have either the marketing orientation or operation management experience to handle the unique challenges of a turnaround.

It could also be argued that certain type of companies such as OEM suppliers or contract manufacturers require CEOs, with techno-engineering skills, but unless the candidate has some understanding about how to get business and/or retain customers and displays some of the above-mentioned attributes, he/she will flop. Trust me.

A Chartered Financial Analyst (CFA) as a CEO

In the very short term, in all turnaround scenarios, the focus has to be on increasing revenue streams and better cash management.

The first means finding a market niche for the company's products and services, while the future strategy is worked out and implemented.

Better cash management requires elimination of wasteful expenses and negotiations with banks and suppliers for more favourable terms. This task often appears to be easier and becomes the immediate priority.

Consequently, the temptation is to put a finance man in charge in a turnaround initiative. After all, the primary task in rebuilding a sick company is to improve operating cash flows, and who is better than a good finance man to cut costs and eliminate wasteful expenditure?

It is also true that restructuring efforts may in time include selling of non-performing assets and non-core businesses, and CFAs will be very valuable as and when these bridges need to be crossed.

But these decisions take time. So does capital restructuring, the objective of which is to expand the equity base, reduce debt and reschedule interest and debt repayment commitments. Experience suggests that capital restructuring efforts are more successful when the company is actually producing better operating results, thus giving investors more confidence.

This however emphasizes the wrong priorities. The turnaround would only be successful when *the business is able to expand the base of satisfied customers*, generating more business and profits. That will be the time when a CFA can bring his skill sets to bear.

A Marketing Man as a CEO

As Theodore Levitt reminds all business managers in 'The Marketing Imagination', 'Without customers, no amount of engineering wizardry, clever financing, or operations expertise can keep the company going. To be the low-cost producer of vacuum tubes, to have the best salesmen of what's not wanted or wanted only by the few whose ability to pay won't even pay for the overhead-these can't save you from extinction. To do well what should not be done is to do badly'.

Peter Drucker says it more succinctly: 'Because its (the corporation) purpose is to create a customer, the business enterprise has two- and only two-basic functions: marketing and innovation. Marketing and innovation produce results; all the rest are "costs"'.

An experienced finance manager can certainly make a significant contribution to controlling costs, but as a CEO will be inappropriate. Unless he has a vision for the business, and is exceptionally talented, he will not be able to spot market opportunities and exploit them to generate revenues.

That apart there is a real danger that across the board cuts will be implemented without paying enough attention to potential long-term damage. This may leave the company too crippled to ever make a comeback. The short-lived benefits of quick cuts have been known to lead to a downward spiral that has been referred to as the 'Anorexia Nervosa'. Companies suffering from this keep cutting costs and end up in an irredeemable morass.

Irrespective of the industry, a marketing person, with venture management or new product development experience, is more likely to be the successful turnaround CEO. Such a person is focused on maximizing opportunities in a wide range of market segments, and is conditioned to take speedy action. He is also familiar with the overall business disciplines, having headed a mini business unit. Above all, he will have been trained to develop resource-led strategies. With adequate support from an able finance director, he can be very effective.

While searching for a marketing professional, another common error, to confuse marketing with sales, needs to be avoided. In many countries, where the information database is weak, and distribution networks are underdeveloped, often, sales managers, because of knowledge based on dealer contacts in many cities and towns, are credited with business acumen in terms of understanding the consumer that they do not necessarily possess. This is the case in most African and a number of Asian countries.

Sales managers' expertise really lies in implementation of marketing policies rather than in devising product and market strategies.

This is not a new revelation. John Z. DeLorean recalls that during his days as the head of Chevrolet division of General Motors, a turnaround situation, General Motors marketing was the least sophisticated in the automobile industry. He said, 'Most American companies today see their contact sales effort as only one part of an overall marketing program. GM sees the sales program as the marketing program. Where modern industry prepares an overall marketing strategy which scientifically ascertains consumer needs, designs products to fill those needs and then merchandises these products to bring the need, the product and the consumer together, GM relied on little more than rah-rah sales pitches and hard-sell techniques'.

This is not to say that sales managers will never develop to become CEOs, they will, but a unidimensional experience is always a handicap.

Industry Background

It is not necessary that that the new CEO has any prior industry experience. While prior experience in the same industry reduces the learning time, prior exposure also results in too ready an acceptance of the business boundaries.

What is necessary is that the new CEO has spent some time in a successful, disciplined and process-driven company and is totally conversant with digital management tools and applications thereof.

The more important issue is his track record. Has he been effective in the basics of any business—increase revenue and control costs? This is easier to determine if the candidate is heading a division, the results of which are often separately reported. In large corporations, often, individual contributions are difficult to assess and the inquiries need to be directed to others in the organization. These have to be fairly focused and will go well beyond standard references.

If he comes from a company culture that values cost-effectiveness, it is important to understand whether he has internalized these values. Even directors of the largest consumer products corporation in India travel economy class in domestic flights. This reflects a strong work ethic. But some senior managers from this company have been known to spend large sums on personal comfort when they move to other companies. Obviously, the value system has not been internalized.

Has he displayed courage of conviction, fought for big ideas and stubbed a few bureaucratic toes in the process? Is he committed? Has he at least one success under his belt? Has he shown willingness to take risks? Has he volunteered for tough assignments displaying a hunger for challenge?

If the answer is yes to all of the above-mentioned questions, you have found your CEO.

CHAPTER 10

PEOPLE MATTER
THE TURNAROUND ORGANIZATION

A successful company is one which has a clear vision, resources and the organization to implement the strategies and plans emerging from the vision.

A start-up CEO begins with a clear vision, strategy and a plan. He/she then raises the financial resources and commences operations with the leanest organization possible, often with one or two trusted aides, and hires more people as and when absolutely necessary.

A smoothly running company has all the pieces in place. A new CEO, mostly promoted from within, will definitely have an agenda for change, but these changes are unlikely to be radical. Incremental changes will be preferred as these do not rock the boat, and are more readily accepted by the organization, especially if such changes are introduced over a period of time.

A company in distress has none of the above. It is confused about its vision, very tight on financial resources and its organization is in disarray, with a weak leader at the top, a demoralized management team hamstrung in a traditional hierarchical command structure and ridiculed by an equally disgruntled underutilized workforce.

It has to begin at the very beginning, without the flexibility of a green field operation.

The journey begins with the induction of a new turnaround CEO.

The new CEO's early days are in a fluid state. A vision has to evolve, resources have to be found and the organization needs to be revamped.

We have discussed in earlier chapters as to how constraints dictate a turnaround CEO's vision and limit his/her options to asset utilization-based strategies.

To add to his woes, the CEO also inherits a hierarchical organization, which is probably moribund by the time he comes on board.

If the CEO had worked for a hierarchical company earlier, he/she would know that an inherent problem with such organizations is that it promotes a 'follow the leader' cult. One who follows blindly is rated highly and rewarded. Despite having to mouth how the company promotes a 'leadership' culture in public, hierarchy bosses are afraid of potential leaders upsetting their applecart, and ensure that any one deviating from the 'follower' regime is moved out of 'harm's' way. The probability of finding managers willing to take any initiative in this scenario will be too much to expect, especially if the CEO also discovers, a very likely scenario, that the more capable senior managers have already moved on to greener pastures.

He/she can then only hope that some of the managers in the next couple of levels down, have more potential than what they have been allowed to show in a hierarchy-bound organization, known to throttle initiatives in the bud. Hopefully, they will step up to the plate because, absent management bandwidth, execution fiascos will destroy the best laid strategies and plans.

Along with the physical assets, the CEO must also audit the skills and capabilities of key individuals, the organization as an entity, as well as the systems and procedures in place.

In any midsize company, the turnaround CEO is likely to find a hierarchical organization structure in place, with a number of VP level executives heading departments operating as virtual silos, drifting further apart from each other, as the floundering predecessor, progressively lost respect and control.

Probably, the best way for the new CEO to land running in his new job, is to send some detailed questionnaires to the VPs, prior to his joining, asking for presentations to be made on day one of his new job. Being new to the company, and probably the industry too, the CEO's questions will perforce be qualitative, with a view to understand the mindsets of the key managers. This will also help the new CEO assess who among the existing lot can be relied upon to begin a transformation journey, and who needs to be removed or replaced.

The meetings should be held separately with each department with the VP and his/her next two levels of managers. The VP will probably need to be encouraged to let some of the junior managers talk.

The purpose is to probe knowledge of the industry and its trends, key success factors required to stay ahead of competition, environmental factors affecting the industry, the talent pool available in the industry and so on. The more aware the managers are of the broader picture, the better.

Next is to get an understanding of the managers' take on the predicament the company has got into. What is the competitive scenario, and how do the company and the competition stand vis-à-vis the key success factors? When did the decline begin? What has your department done to arrest the slide? How have competitors weathered the storm? Is the declining trend reversible? What are your suggestions? What should the company focus on?

And then on to specifics: do you have the domain knowledge? What are your competitive strengths? Are you passionate about what you do? Do you have all the people you need? Do you have productive people? Are the people happy? What have you done to improve skill sets in your department? Do you have a training plan and schedule? How do you manage interdepartmental interactions? At which level? Formally, through structured meetings or informally as and when needed?

I recommend that the new CEO should spend enough time in learning the systems and processes in place. Is information gathering and processing digitized and real-time? How many are computer literate? Can I see the output reports? What is the decision-making process—is it based on data and analytics? How much do you value experience and gut feel? Are plans made for the week, the month or the quarter? How often are plans reviewed and by whom? Are meetings planned ahead, agendas circulated and meetings minuted?

Then the hard questions, perhaps best excluded from the advance questionnaire. Who is responsible for the current state of affairs in the company? Which department? Do we have competent people everywhere? How many extra people do we have? Can we rightsize the company?

The questions will vary department to department. Finance needs to be asked compliance questions as well as processes for setting and monitoring budgets. Sales need to be grilled about the database of potential customers and processes in place for reaching out to them, and getting feedback. Marketing needs to be asked whether they see themselves as the driving force of the company and how do they perform this role and so on.

The Turnaround Organization Structure

Restructuring an existing organization is always more difficult than creating a new organization, especially in a turnaround, where the organizational structure will differ from a hierarchical company in fundamental ways.

The CEO, for example, cannot afford to remain locked in an ivory tower. He/she must get involved in all aspects of the business and provide leadership at various levels and ensure linkages at all points. The primary task is to make the company work as a team, sharing authority and responsibility to achieve common goals.

This is best achieved by adopting a matrix structure.

While restructuring, some internal and external realities need to be factored in.

The interaction with various departments and managers would have given the new CEO some insight into the core competencies of the company's senior management and the quality of the talent available within. With some luck, the CEO would also have spotted a few second line managers eager to take on more responsibilities. They can be nurtured to become the 'change agents' the company so desperately needs. Almost always there will be some under-performing VPs who will need underpinning by domain experts brought in from outside.

The problem of hiring talent from outside gets exacerbated when the company's image gets weakened by media reports on its 'losses'. The inability to pay top dollar further hampers its efforts to induct outside change agents. Hopefully, the CEO's contacts and personal reputation will help.

Development of Talent from Within

Perforce the turnaround CEO will have to depend heavily on the talents and skills available within the company.

This is not necessarily a daunting prospect. No company ever loses all their knowledge and skill custodians. The challenge is to spot them in the maze of the present organization, pull them out and place them in positions where they can be effective. Somewhat rusty they may be, but, these are the people who will form the core team of change agents, who will help the CEO begin the transformation journey in earnest.

They will certainly need some refresher courses to contemporize their domain knowledge and skill sets, as well as hone up on their interpersonal skills, an essential element in a matrix organization.

Identifying reorientation and training needs for the chosen few, and implementing a continuous and rigorous training regime for them, therefore, become an urgent priority for the new CEO. Fortunately, there are many training institutes and professionals who can design and conduct focused training programmes. These will cost money, but will be an investment for the future.

In a company, training sessions not only send positive signals across the company, but also provide a forum for introducing changes in work practice and culture. An added benefit is the opportunity to identify more change agents to join the core team.

Irrespective, the turnaround CEO should maintain a wish list of talent and continue the search for them for induction into the company as and when possible. The enlarged talent pool will have their hands full as the company moves forward and gets ready to look beyond immediate survival.

Redefining Key Functions

Peter Drucker's succinct verdict on this topic is worth restating: 'Because the corporations purpose is to create a customer, the business enterprise has two, and only two basic functions: marketing and innovation: all the rest are costs'.

Marketing understands the customers' need and prepares a theoretical construct of a product (or service) which will satisfy their need. R&D (innovation) then adds flesh and blood to the product concept. Marketing then persuades the customer to buy the product, in preference to competitive products, for a price which yields a satisfactory level of profit for the company.

There are many more support functions between the mind and the market, without which no transaction can be completed. Raw materials/components have to be bought, products need to be produced/assembled, packed and delivered to the customer.

Procurement (supply chain), manufacturing, quality control, packaging and delivery (logistics) are the key functions as well, along with, what I call back-office functions such as HR and finance. None of these functions generate revenue or profits on their own, but incur costs to reach the product to the customers and are best judged by how efficient they are in keeping the costs down.

A number of very successful businesses actually thrive only with marketing and innovations and a rudimentary accounts department, for example, Apple, one of the most valuable companies in the world for the longest time. Apple shows the customer what he needs, designs a product to dazzle, gets the customer to queue up overnight in front of an Apple dealer to be able to pick up the latest device fresh off the docks having made the journey from a third-party contract manufacture located half way across the world.

Many start-ups would love to adopt this model, but not having the scale cannot build an outsourcing support system and hence, they are forced into setting up own facilities to manufacture. Once a respectable scale is reached, manufacturing and all other functions can be outsourced, for example Dell, Levi's, Ikea and brand extensions—Armani suits to watches, Prada dresses to shoes, Louis Vuitton from luggage to fashion accessories, Davidoff from cigarettes to aftershave lotions and the list is endless.

In stark contrast, the turnaround CEO, in a midsize company, is probably going to be lumbered with weak marketing and innovation, and other grossly overmanned and under-performing departments.

The CEO needs to get a strong marketing and an innovation person on board ASAP, paying whatever it takes.

He needs to then impress on the other departmental heads that *they are the cost centres* and they will be judged by how they improve productivity and thereby reduce cost per piece, with quantitative, time-bound targets. Some attainable goals for an under-performing company, and negotiable even with the most intransigent unions, are as follows:

- get it right first time, on time, every time;
- retrain workforce;
- eliminate process and material wastage;
- eliminate machine downtime;
- produce more than machine-rated capacity;
- reuse and recycle and
- reduce energy and water consumption.

Routine back room functions such as HR, admin, skill development, retraining and new skill training should be outsourced immediately.

The so-called key HR functions such as annual reviews, appraisals and promotions should revert back to departmental heads and be driven by merit and not quotas.

The Wired-in Organization

In today's world, no business can survive unless it is able to make informed decisions, which means real-time data collection, processing, assimilation and analytics of the company's own operations and digitization of the entire process.

Neither can it survive without real-time awareness of external influences on the business, such as the future drivers of change, the new frontiers opened up by globalization, the new intensity of cross-border competition, the heightened environmental consciousness, the present society's expectations from the business community at large and the company's products and services in particular, the employees' expectations from the workplace and above all, the expectations of the new millennium customer.

The CEO, fortunately, today, can have digital systems installed which collet, collate and deliver all relevant information as and when needed.

A useful by-product of the data-processing applications is the ability to monitor individual performances. State Bank of India recently announced that the performance review system of all frontline personnel will give 70 per cent weightage to the transaction efficiency of each individual, as each transaction is now digitized. The other obvious benefit is to be able to communicate to everyone in the company via e-mail, and with customers, suppliers and so on through the website.

The CEO can also keep communication lines open at all levels through e-mail, thus bypassing structural barriers.

If the turnaround CEO finds that his company has not invested in adequate computer linkages, and that there is a low level of comfort in such 'high tech' concepts within the company, especially among the older managers who have decided that the traditional and systems are more adequate, he must set that right.

Computerization of information is expensive. But it pays for itself in many ways—helping make quick and correct data-supported decisions, reducing supervisory headcount, accelerating transition to an inclusive work culture, eliminating duplication of work, increasing productivity and finally reducing waste by keeping a hawk eye on expenses vis-à-vis budgets.

Project Management Orientation

Typically, in a venture management model, a project is assigned to a full-time project manager. The project manager starts off with a small, multi-discipline team. The core team is progressively expanded with inside and outside resources to eventually take on the aspect of an independent company as the business takes off. Large corporations such as 3M, General Mills and many others have effectively used this model in planning their new product development and diversification projects.

Such task and task force focus can be equally effective in the turnaround process.

Cross-functional project groups can be used in various scenarios, be it in launching new products or addressing cost reduction or finding new distribution outlets.

The project manager, having got a clear definition of the problem, examines the possible solutions. Thereafter, having got the CEO' and the senior managements' agreement on a course of action, he firms up on strategy, plans resource deployment and supervises the implementation of the plan. He will also establish milestones and review and report the progress at predetermined intervals. With the right calibre, the project manager and a reasonable support team, the CEO and the senior management only need to monitor that a balance is maintained between planning and creative freedom given to the project team, and keep themselves free to tackle other issues.

In the early days of a turnaround, the company is really faced with the task of solving a series of problems, and the organization best geared to succeed is the one that recognizes that and structures itself accordingly. If each problem is a project, then the project manager's approach is the most apt. It follows therefore that the turnaround organization is most effective if it can structure itself as a series of project groups, which are pulled together at the very top.

This in turn results in a flat matrix that ensures sharing of goals and information, complementing mutual skills, quicker decision-making and more efficient monitoring of the progress made.

The success of the project groups will be determined by its constitution. It must have a competent project manager as the catalyst. The project teams must have representation from each of the concerned departments. Each representative will in turn be able to draw on the combined wisdom of his department whenever required. He should also be empowered to commit his department's compliance to the tasks required by the project group.

As the company's ability to recover from its present plight will be determined entirely by the market' response to how it plans and positions its products and services, the project group needs to be market led. That does not mean that each project group has a marketing man as the project leader. But the project leader must at all times be aware and responsive to market needs.

For example, if the company identifies an opportunity in reducing outer packaging costs, it cannot just be the buyer going out to buy thinner ply outer cartons. The buyer may be the appropriate project leader, but logistics need to be happy with the ease of handling the size, shape and weight of the carton and its strength to undertake the number of required journeys. Sales need to ensure that any customer reuse value of the existing carton is not totally eroded; if that is unavoidable, an alternate compensation for the buyer has to be planned. Finance needs to work out financial models to determine at which point additional damage in transit resulting from using lighter cartons sets off the savings. Marketing should assess the impact on customer goodwill if the retailers have to handle higher breakages. And the buyer has to ensure dependable supply sources.

Let's look at a somewhat more complex scenario.

Turnaround CEOs are at times faced with unexpected surprises. The company he has joined turns out to have some assets and people left over from the days when the company was engaged in diverse activities, with a tenuous link with the primary business. HMV (refer Chapter 2), a Kolkata-based music company, had set up a large carpentry shop to make hand-cranked record players, which the company marketed at low prices to promote the sale of their records and it was a good marketing move at the time, but now an albatross, as the market had moved on to electronic record players with entertainment hardware companies taking over the market.

The company was now saddled with more than 100 workers in the shop, who had earlier rejected VRSs, and with full backing of the workers' union kept showing up every day and collected their pay cheques at the end of the month. In between, they did no work.

This was one of the smaller problems I had to face. The workers' union secretary made it clear in a couple of one-on-one meetings I had with him, that there is no way a separation scheme can be worked out with these workers. But, I pointed out to him, that this unit had no relevance to our business any more. He agreed and shrugged. I further pointed out to him that the machines and tools are well past their use-by date and cannot be made productive. 'How do you know?' he asked, and said you give them some work and see how good the machines are.

I agreed to scout for some furniture-making business and asked in return, what happens if the customers reject the produce. He said, you get the business and we will see. He then said he will personally supervise the work done, and if the unit fails to deliver he will make the workers accept a retirement scheme.

Sometimes turnaround strategies evolve from such outré situations! This was the ideal time to put a project management team in place.

The way forward was to hire a business development manager (BDM), who promptly got an order from a local Taj Hotel to build a demo cupboard for a bedroom. The cupboard was cleared on quality, but the price on offer was ridiculously low, not even covering the cost of the wood!

Eventually, the BDM got an export order for some bedside tables at a good price. I was told by my labour relations manager that the union secretary was standing on a crate in the carpentry shop exhorting the workers to work faster and better. The appearance of the union secretary on the shop floor, that too day after day, was a surprise to all and sundry.

The consignment was shipped on time and the BDM was ecstatic. As luck would have it, the whole consignment was rejected.

I must say to the credit of the union secretary that he convinced the workers to accept the retirement scheme. They did, when we had put together enough money to pay the separation package.

We repeated a similar exercise for the workers of the record pressing plant, a few weeks later. We used the vinyl record pressing machines to make Melmoware dinner plates and PVC flanges for pipelines in acid-producing plants. We did not how to market them!

But the union secretary took pity on me and persuaded these workers to accept a retirement plan as well.

The project management did deliver in the end.

The Board's Role in the Restructuring Process

The CEO should have total freedom in selecting his core team. The board needs to ensure that.

The board needs to extend full co-operation in supporting the CEO implement the necessary changes. The CEO's judgement in contentious issues arising from rightsizing, which may require extensive changes at the top, and diligence in his choice of replacements, both from within and outside the company, has to be accepted. If the board has likely replacement candidates in mind, suggestions can be made, but that's where it must stop. This is particularly relevant for companies in which a single owner or a family has controlling shares. The board must protect the CEO from undue pressures from such quarters.

Many company boards including multi-nationals insist that heads of finance and marketing are appointed in consultation with them. This is probably a good practice in a start-up, but not so for a turnaround. The turnaround CEO must be totally comfortable with his team. He has to share a vision with them, and he is therefore likely to select managers who, at least appear to share the same values with him and have similar goals in life. He also needs total loyalty and will not have time to deal with the inevitable politics that result from having managers working for him, who believe there is a hotline to the board, because their final appointment was cleared by the board.

The board also needs to understand that the CEO is unlikely to get the best team in place on day one. He will need to fill a few positions quickly and may have to settle for a few who don't match up to his standards. Some will grow to their jobs. Some won't. The CEO will get rid of them as soon as he can.

Changes in personnel should not be construed as mistakes, but taken for what they are—expedient decisions that needed to be made at a point of time. If a turnaround CEO has to wait for a Mr Right, he may have to wait forever.

CHAPTER 11

CORE VALUES OF A COMPANY

WINNING WITH GRACE

Richard Branson, the chairman of Virgin Atlantic, said: 'We strongly urge you to fly British Airways on April 23. As for the other 364 days of the year, you will still find the best fares and best service on Virgin Atlantic'.[1]

Why would anyone urge you to fly a competitor's airline, that too barely a month after the end of the First Gulf War when allied troops led by the United States freed Kuwait from Iraqi occupation, a war which had triggered an air passenger traffic drop by as much as 30 per cent?

Most carriers made steep cuts in fares in a combined knee-jerk reaction, but alas, seats continued to remain empty as people stayed away from flying because of 'fear of terrorism'.

That's when British Airways' (BA) combative culture came to the surface, a culture they had inculcated among all their employees a few years ago when BA was facing near bankruptcy.

They sidestepped conventional wisdom and prudent financial practices, and announced a lottery in 67 countries giving away

---

[1] *Source*: New York Times, 22 March, 1991.

50,000 seats on its international flights on April 23 to Britain, and any return date before 31 May to the winners. Even seats aboard the Concorde would be free!

Lord King, the BA Chairman said in a press meet, 'The engine of consumer demand did not just idle in neutral, it sputtered to a complete stop during the Gulf war' and 'now it needs a kick start'.

The 50,000 tickets would represent an estimated $18 million, in lost revenues, and perhaps a tenth of that as operating margins. A notional figure and a *transient asset*, which gainfully employed could put the fliers back into the flying habit.

Judging from the thousands of people who swamped BA's reservation centres on Regent Street in London, and 65 other cities across the world, this promotion was a triumph of the 'can do' culture of BA.

What is Company Culture?

There is no one definition of company culture. It is probably best described as a blend of the value system the promoter/owner would have had in mind when starting the business.

'If I make the best mousetrap, customers would queue up in front of my door' is a palpably different value system from the one which asks whether customers are bothered by rodent infestation and can I do something useful for them? And then, one proceeds to market a solution.

As an organization grows, its culture evolves, shaped by, among others by its history, product range, the market niche it occupies, technology, its risk appetite, the type of employees it attracts and retains, but above all, the leadership style of the CEO. Eventually, the culture determines the boldness of the company's vision, the strategies it adopts, the systems it puts in place, the self-belief it promotes and the confidence with which it handles adversities.

It was BA's culture, its DNA, which allowed it to come up with a bold and innovative strategy to pull the market out of the depths of 'despair', when its competitors, lacking a combative, winning culture came up with conventional and far less effective responses to the same crisis.

FACTORS THAT DETERMINE COMPANY CULTURE

There are a number of factors that shape a company's culture. The influence of each element is not uniformly equal in all organizations. Had it been so, all companies would have had a universal culture, no matter where they operate.

- The political environment, social values, industrial policies, 'ease of doing business', access to capital and skilled workforce, the tax regime and so on are a few of the factors which influence company cultures. In a controlled economy, 'expertise in environment management', meaning influencing the government of the day, is a key success factor. By definition, a company more adept in appeasing the greed of corrupt officials fares better in such scenarios. The culture of a company thriving in this climate will be very different from an open market milieu, where business acumen, other than paying bribes, is the key success factor.
- The nature of the industry and its location play significant roles. Companies with exclusive mining rights in remote areas are more prone to adopt autocratic and exploitative styles of management than those in more competitive industries in urban areas where employee mobility is greater.
- The technology and the products and services the company offers often explains the difference in cultures in smokestack industries and say, IT industries. The more modern the technology employed the more dynamic the company's culture is axiomatic.
- The customer's ability to make informed choices, the quality of competition, media reach, acceptance of fair play as a social value and awareness of the impact on the earth, are a few more important factors that shape a company's culture.

These factors would have determined the company's history and tradition, which in effect resulted in its present culture. Except that dominant leaders leave indelible influences on the evolution of the company's culture, irrespective of the factors discussed above.

Henry Ford's single-minded devotion to mass production, Jamsetji Tata's vision for a smokestack industry, Harold S. Geneen's faith in diversification through acquisitions and Akio Morita's dedication to miniaturization, to name a few, are examples of one man's thinking determining the organizational bias towards innovation which have determined the cultures of very large corporations.

Such leaders delineate the company's goals, values and beliefs. Policy guidelines regarding the organization—its structure and its flexibility, operating procedures, information and control norms and reward and measurement systems were laid down by them to have eventually become the bulwark on which the culture evolved. All companies, big and small, have such visionaries to drive the business at some stage.

In the last 30 years or so, consumer power has emerged as the most potent influence on the company's culture. The customer not only decides what the company should make but how it goes about making it. Levi's loses business in the United States when the customer decides that Levi's is exploiting child labour and not paying fare wages to their employees in some of the Asian and Latin American countries. The safety features in most cars are the result of one man's crusade against an unsafe car.

HOW DOES A COMPANY SHAPE ITS CULTURE?

Disneyland and McDonald's

A trip to any one of the Disney amusement parks makes one wonder how Disney creates an ambience of *happiness* as if it's a magic potion distilled and bottled by the company which the visitors unknowingly imbibe as they enter through the turnstile.

A day at a Disney park takes hours. If you enter at 10 in the morning, you will wonder whether the 10 hours have gone, when the park shuts at 8 pm for the night. Even then some of the rides will remain untaken, some of the castles unvisited.

Do the rides take 10 hours? If it was timed, all the rides together will barely take an hour.

What happens in between? The visitor stands in, what would be in any other circumstances, interminable queues. But the point is that in Disneyland the queues are not interminable; they are in fact as enjoyable interludes between the rides as the rides themselves. It's that magic air of happiness which will keep you smiling and laughing and pleasantly bantering with others in the queue, equally unfazed about having to wait for every ride.

But the businessman knows that Disney has not 'manufactured' the magic air. What they have really done is set up a few standards—standards of cleanliness, standards of apparent friendliness, standards for fixed smiles and polite talk, standards of unobtrusive security and a schedule of parades and other pleasant diversions between standing in queues.

The standards are infectious. Visitors do not shout or scream in frustration, they do not call Mickey Mouse an aging midget, they do not jump queues and they travel the extra few yards to find a bin. They help each other, share fries and corn dogs and forget to ogle at anyone. They don't kick little brats or curse their parents for bringing them along. Amazingly, even the brats do not behave as brats.

What Disneyland exudes is the Disney culture. They go to great lengths to inculcate it among its employees, their own mini society, who in turn pass it on to the bigger society, the millions and millions that enter the Disney parks every year.

Will this be relevant to other businesses?

McDonald's say yes.

McDonald's has no pretensions of being anything other than a fast food joint. The interiors are bright and cheerful. The menu is limited. Burgers and fries are not high up in the healthy food category. They don't even serve you at the table; on top of that you are expected to clear your own table after you finish.

But, over the years it has remained a good place to go to with or without the kids, with or without the girlfriend, on the way to work, at the lunch break, before or after a movie, for a snack and the all American feel good ambience, that pull people back in time after time. Why?

They also have their unvarying standards. The serving counter is clean; so is the partial view of the kitchen. The girl or the boy at the counter has a smart unstained uniform, a ready smile, a chirpy 'and how are you today' on the lips, willingness to look you in the eye and quick in giving you change and your order without ever hurrying you. As you move on, the eating counters are clean, a spilled coffee or ice cream quietly swept up, toddlers helped into their chairs and if you want to visit the rest rooms they are spotless.

McDonald's has been able to replicate the same ambience in whichever country they have opened up in, irrespective of the crowd behaviour norms in these countries.

The Disney and the McDonald's examples suggest that the culture of a company is perhaps best understood as its customary and 'traditional' way of thinking and doing things. To remain successful, they no doubt work very hard to maintain their customary way of doing things. That centres on their ability to make 'the way' which is eminently acceptable to all employees. All new employees must absorb the culture and radiate it to whoever they come in contact with.

These processes in fact are their *core values*.

VALUE STATEMENTS

Many companies having realized that they lack a uniform culture have sought a vehicle to promote work cultures and shared values among its employees.

A very useful tool to promote a positive work culture is to seek an ISO standards certification, or its equivalent in the industry.

It forces the CEO and the top management to debate and agree on a vision for the company—a realistic goal, given the company's present position in the market, its resources and its organization structure. It further disciplines the top management to agree on a set of objectives—both qualitative and quantitative, and determine the process by which these objectives will be met.

The processes are then set out as mission statements, often displayed in prominent positions in the workplace, to help each employee understand the objectives of the organization and the role of each employee in the overall scheme of things.

The management hopes that constant reminders about the recommended ways of doing things will percolate down, be internalized and become the core value system of the company.

If such statements are pious platitudes emphasizing heavily, and vaguely 'what the company would like to be' rather than 'what is', they get what they deserve—little support. People Express Airlines once stated that the airline's purpose was to 'become the leading institution for constructive change in the world'. Inspirational to the average employee? Not likely.

On the other hand, if it is an honest appraisal of the company and it sets out 'what is' leading to 'what can be' it will be taken more seriously and will actually pose a positive challenge to its employees to achieve the corporate goals.

Bell Atlantic's vision statement in 'To be the customer's first choice for communication and information services in every market we serve, domestic and international' is an interesting contrast to People Express Airlines. It is clear about their business—communication and information services, their aspiration—to be the customer's first choice and the domain—domestic and international markets.

It brings product focus, it acknowledges the competitiveness of the market and it underlines globalization. Thereby it gives direction to the entire company, keep abreast, if not ahead, of technology, stay tuned to customer service needs and exploit opportunities wherever they open up.

Another successful organization, Marriott Corporation and their staff are equally clear about Marriott's goals. The mission states 'Marriott is committed to being the best lodging and food service in the world by treating employees in a way that create extraordinary customer service and shareholder value'. Not only is it clear, but it also tells the employees how integral they are to achieving the corporate goal, and at the same time reminds each one of his responsibilities to the corporation and its major constituencies.

Eddie Bauer Holdings, a US chain of upmarket outdoor and casual clothes and gear, has recovered from bankruptcy a few years ago. Their core values remained steadfast through the years of turmoil.

The company's creed 'to give outstanding quality, value, service and guarantee that we may be worthy of you esteem', articulated by its founder, has been the guiding force of the company.

Eddie Bauer also knows that honest dealing is a key element in creating lifetime customers, and the company policy is derived from this knowledge. 'Doing business with integrity has long been an understood part of Eddie Bauer's culture. Integrity is a value intrinsic to our company's success and our company is committed to promoting an environment of integrity. Each and every associate is accountable to these high standards'.[2]

Eddie Bauer spends little time on training a new inductee, 'an associate' before he is asked to interact with customers in one of their stores. The mission statement comes alive to the new trainee, on the job, as the store manager and the other more experienced assistants constantly refer to the prominently displayed mission statement 'Our business environment is one of integrity and respect for our customers, for our associates and the communities in which we do business'.

They equally proudly display an ethics statement, 'communicate in all instances with candour and accurate, forthright information' and to 'avoid actions which personally benefit ourselves'. The transparent enthusiasm of the associates reassures the customer that he knows what he is buying and he is only buying what he wants, and not a line on which the associate gets incentive remuneration.

---

[2] *Source*: Company website.

Sharing Goals and Dreams—Information Flow

The switch to a culture of openness, sharing information through frequent town hall meetings in most tech savvy companies has happened owing to the negative value of using information as a power base in traditional companies.

For a long time in the history of corporations, general information about the company, its performance, its aspirations and its future plans, were closely held secrets among senior managers. A number of old timers still believe in the 'need to know' principle, while sharing information. Many CEOs are guilty of keeping senior managers in the dark as well, forcing each department to second guess what others were up to, in the process creating an environment of suspicion and resultant insecurity.

An inevitable fallout of such tactics is that each division, and sometimes each department within the division, develops a subculture of its own, trying to protect its operations from prying eyes, and keeping outside, meaning other departments, interactions to the minimum.

Inevitably, territorial jealousy creates individual power centres, each with its own agenda. Such an environment militates against fostering uniform attitudes towards job skills and technical knowledge, discipline and punishment, the values placed on different kinds of work, the relationships it builds with customers and suppliers, the decision-making process (democratic or dictatorial) and appreciation of new thoughts, in essence the ingredients that create the company culture. If anything, it creates talent mismatches in key functions. A strong marketing team has poor products to sell, or a strong R&D team gets frustrated by the lukewarm approach of the sales force in peddling new products.

Transformation of Culture in an Under-performing Company

The passive acceptance of impending doom is the biggest challenge facing a turnaround CEO. Damages caused by external threats have already happened. Competitors have taken the business away, facilities have become 'obsolete', and good people have been poached. The environment becomes more threatening as global players offer better and cheaper products, more freely available in markets forced to lift cross-border trade restrictions.

If the company is to revive, a change in the mindset of the middle managers and the office staff would be the starting point. They would be insecure and resist changes. Of greater concern would be their cynicism, their refusal to accept that a rescue operation is possible. This will manifest itself in infuriating responses—it cannot be done, that's not the way it works, we have tried it before.

Groups will form to resist introduction of efficient systems and processes. To them, the fear of redundancy is real. Other groups will try their best to get close to the new CEO, through backbiting and complaining against others.

Only a very few will lend genuine support to the changes. They need to be spotted early, protected and nursed into change agents.

The second cultural challenge lies in integrating the workforce into the mainstream. Workers, contrary to conventional management wisdom, are actually more attuned to work. They are familiar with accountability as their contribution is more easily measurable, even to themselves, and they feel more vulnerable if the company is doing badly. They see declining sales and mounting inventories for what they are—a lead up to fall in production—and disappearance of their jobs and income. They have seen too many closures, lay-offs and lockouts not to believe that their livelihood is at stake.

Their apprehensions need to be allayed. The value of retraining and reskilling to face present day challenges has to be *sold* to the workmen. Routine communication will not be enough.

Tools for Culture Transformation

The turnaround manager, faced with the task of transforming a sick company has to begin by questioning and rewriting some of the basic convictions that will enable acceptance of a new set of values and beliefs. But the communication to the company of the changes will have to be through external manifestations of the transformation happening deep down.

The abolition of hierarchical structures, team approach to solving problems and greater access to decision-makers need to be visible down the line.

This begins with the CEO making an attempt to be more visible and accessible through regular walkabouts in offices and shop floors, stopping to interact with one or a group of employees, helping and so on.

Physical layouts of offices have to change. Closed cabins with secretaries guarding the doors will have to go. Changing to an open plan office sends signals that hierarchies are no longer sacred and promotes an environment more conducive to teamwork.

A spruced-up office and a landscaped factory make coming to work more pleasant and lift morale. Installation of modern technology by way of computers and e-mail make the unit more conducive to newer technologies.

Weekly open meetings can initiate the rite of questioning the established order of the organization. A Monday morning stand-up 15-minute meeting at the CEO's office of all senior and middle level managers to discuss this week's key tasks gives opportunities for free expression. Similar meetings down the line, in departmental managers' offices, which the CEO pointedly attends occasionally, will break a lot of barriers.

Inviting outside experts to do critical reports of certain operations and circulating the reports extensively also establish the right to question and fosters constructive internal criticism.

Reinstating a few common activities in a low-morale environment sends signals of hope. Annual picnics, impromptu get-togethers to celebrate crossing a milestone or solving a tricky problem or even putting up a sign board that records yesterday's production and sales promote not only fellow feeling but a commitment to do better.

Ensuring that any communication from the company is well designed and produced—from letterheads and envelopes to product brochures, sales manuals and annual reports—signals a change to quality consciousness that will eventually rub off on production units.

These if supported by more formal processes, like employee opinion surveys and job redesigning programmes based on these surveys, will institutionalize the renewal programme.

Similarly, programmes to facilitate changes in social roles and status have long-term impact. Training programmes for all levels, especially in-house training programmes do not cost a lot, but give a sense of purpose and fulfilment to both trainers and trainees. Retirement tea parties give other employees a sense of good feeling. Induction programmes help people fit in faster and be more productive quicker.

The sensitive turnaround manager finds many more such tools. A managing director cutting a cake or distributing sweets to workmen when an order is executed on time is often remembered more fondly than a small monetary incentive.

The case of the Tehri Dam completion is a good example of how the culture transformation task can be made less daunting than it is often made out to be.

Tehri Dam on the Bhagirathi River near Tehri in Uttarakhand, the tallest in India and one of the tallest in the world, was commissioned in early 2007; a good 30 years after construction had begun.

The Tehri Hydro Development Corporation was formed in 1988, with assured funds from the central and state governments, to manage the dam, after its technical and financial project partner USSR declared its inability to honour its financial commitments owing to political problems at home.

In 1990, the project design was changed to create a reservoir for irrigation and generate a 1000 megawatt of power.

Thereafter, a number of disparate issues held the progress of the construction up at various stages. The primary concern was the relocation of 10,000 families in the Tehri village, which would be submerged once the dam was constructed. The second concern was the proposed location, considered vulnerable to very high intensity earthquakes. The third was local sentiment about changing the course of a river considered holy. Consequently, the work ethic in the company was compromised.

A new chairman was appointed in 2004 to speed up the progress, who committed to open the dam by early 2007. He had four priorities: unlock contractual log jams, both with the Russian partners and local civil contractors and vendors; accelerate upgradation of engineering support systems; put the rehabilitation of displaced villagers on a fast track and make the organization task- and time-oriented.

Unlike his predecessor, who was mostly camping in Delhi, the Chairman moved his office to Tehri. The general managers, who were also camping in Delhi along with the previous chairman, had to follow suit.

While the general managers started visiting the site, the new chairman spent the first two months reviewing the job descriptions of every employee and ensuring that each one knew his/her tasks and had a time-bound schedule to follow. Simultaneously, he put an accelerated computerization programme in place along with intensive retraining of the employees to feel at home in a digitized environment.

Once accountability was established, digitization made monitoring easy.

The new chairman then proceeded to make himself both visible and accessible, to all levels, by undertaking regular site visits, having informal shop floor meetings when often foremen led the discussions and of course more structured review meetings with his managers.

The result? Tehri Dam opened for business on the appointed day and hour. Probably, a first for a PSU.

CHAPTER 12

GETTING READY FOR THE FUTURE

SUSTAINABLE SURVIVAL AND GROWTH STRATEGIES

Way back in 2012, Nikkei reported that Japan's Ministry of Economy, Trade and Industry is teaming up with Toyota and other major Japanese manufacturers to develop *technology for recovering and recycling rare earth metals*. It could eventually allow Japan to slash its rare earth imports by at least 10 per cent by 2025. Currently, Japan relies on China for approximately 80 per cent of its rare earth elements.

This report highlights two strategy-linked issues.

The first is the importance of *factor advantage*, articulated by Michael Porter in his book *The Competitive Advantage of Nations*,[1] and the second is being the value in recycling and reuse.

---

[1] Porter, Michael E. 1990. The Competitive Advantage of Nations. New York: Free Press.

The turnaround CEO will know that the only sustainable winning strategy for any company is to try and create an *unfair advantage* over competition.

Historically, factor advantages provided such unfair advantages to the likes of De Beers, who controlled the diamond mines in Africa, or the countries in the Middle East, who owned most of the oil wells in the world. Many Chinese companies are able to swamp export markets with their goods with predatory pricing, because they can leverage volume-driven low-cost capabilities—a result of the factor advantage of a *huge home market* owing to its large population.

The second is *creative asset utilization* strategies—reuse and recycle, being key success factors in such strategies.

Creating Unfair Advantages

The turnaround CEO will find out early enough that his/her company does not have any unutilized physical factor advantages. True, a gold mining company may find that recent spurts in the price of gold have made the cost of mining a fallow mine worthwhile, but then a commodity market does not need a turnaround whiz at the helm of affairs. A more relevant example is that of the profitability of shale oil extractors, in recent times when crude was fetching a US$ 100+ price per barrel. With the price of crude dropping well below that magic figure, the cost of extracting shale oil makes this business unviable, and must go into cold storage, to be revived if and when crude prices go way up north again.

There may be, and often is, in the asset list of distressed companies, some unused land and buildings in prime areas, and subject to mortgage holders' permission, can fetch high rental incomes, but then this is unlikely to be the core business of the company. These may, however, generate some much needed cash, if cleverly handled, but will not remain an unfair advantage over competition.

The turnaround CEO can of course look at new business opportunities with such factor advantages, as the owner of the PVR Cinemas in India, Mr Bijli, did. Presumably, he had the funds to acquire decrepit cinema halls and renovate them to meet the exacting standards of multiplexes all over the world.

In today's business scenarios, increasingly, an unfair advantage over competition is built upon the foundation of intangible assets, ranging from brand equities, patents, copyrights and trademarks to innovation capabilities, process superiorities and fair trade practices. How can an under-performing company create such assets?

A turnaround CEO would have by now determined what business, that is, industry, his/her company is in, and what are the key success factors in this industry. He/she would have also evaluated the residual quality of the assets available for exploitation, and for how long. That apart, there will be clarity on the lack of capabilities responsible for the decline in the company's performance.

Hopefully, he/she would have perused the order book as well, and met up with a few customers who still have some faith in the company.

Loyal customers tend to be more objective about the strengths and the weaknesses of the company than many loyal employees. They are more likely to be appreciative of the company's strengths vis-à-vis its competitors, especially if they have remained loyal to the company's products despite temporary discontinuity in supplies or uneven quality, a baggage that a turnaround manager inherits. They are also likely to be supportive of the company's revival efforts and would provide pointers to immediately productive activities.

The customer interface will enable the turnaround manager to better understand current market realities and give the CEO valuable insights on which products and services can be the best launch pads for mounting the turnaround initiative.

Life Cycle

The selection of the most appropriate business strategy is largely determined by the stage of life cycle of the industry is in, and the company's ability to improve its capabilities to match the needs of the market. The CEO's task becomes clear—identify and nurture the assets and capabilities required to meet the challenges posed by the key success factors.

SUNRISE INDUSTRIES SERVING NASCENT MARKETS

Electric cars are a good example of a nascent or new market. Given the almost universal concern for global warming and the need to reduce carbon emission, the cries for an alternative to petrol or diesel driven cars have been heard for a long time.

All auto majors in the United States, Europe, Japan and Korea have dedicated resources to develop pollution-free electric cars, but by default these remained marginal focus areas.

This segment has been slow to take off largely because of technology inadequacy in increasing charge holding capacity, reducing almost 8 hours of recharge time even for tiny cars and high prices resulting from high capital costs and low outputs. Reva, the first electric car on Indian roads, did not have the staying power and had to sell out to Mahindra, who have not been able to do much with it so far either.

Tesla has begun accepting pre-orders for a spacious Sedan which will run 300 miles (almost 500 km) on one charge, and can be recharged while you have coffee at Starbucks in one of the many Tesla recharge stations coming up soon on major interstate highways.

Tesla is addressing the major problems. Judging from the quarter million car advance orders, the potential customers are not daunted by the relatively high unit price. If Tesla succeeds, it may well change the fate of the electric car, and the destiny of many other companies languishing in this market. Mahindra will benefit when Tesla's success gives this market segment the boost it has been waiting for.

In the last decade, we have also seen the rise and fall of many e-commerce companies, the surviving ones valued at billions of dollars, but yet to make sustained profits, if any, and innumerable ones biting the dust with investors' funds, running into billions as well, going up in smoke.

Turning an under-performing company in a nascent segment must be the toughest assignment a new CEO can bargain for. The task here is to expand the size of the market by acquiring new customers which means speculative high spends in advertising and promotions, requiring large cash resources, which are rarely available in a turnaround scenario.

Perforce the CEO will have to engage in a holding operation, ticking away, till a 'Tesla' comes along to kick-start the growth of the segment of the industry his/her company is in.

MATURE MARKETS

The low or static growth rates deter new entrants. The more agile fringe players exit and the markets are virtually left to one or two major players who adopt essentially milking strategies. The emphasis shifts to improving margins by lowering costs and raising prices, whenever possible. Innovations that could have kick-started market growth are ignored. A result of that is steering a middle course, satisfying most of the needs of most of the customers and leaving specialist gaps. Fierce rivalry, the primary fuel of growing markets, is contained. The players behave as if they have defined boundaries for themselves and appear to leave each other enough room to avoid price wars and technology battles.

A turnaround manager, in such situations has the opportunity of finding at least a temporary competitive advantage by modifying his company's products and services to meet the needs of those customers or market segments neglected by the major players.

However, the distinction between the different phases of market life cycle is not always clear-cut. The same industry can be at different stages of its life cycle in different geographies, and at times among different consumer clusters in the same geography.

FMCG, home appliances and entertainment electronics illustrate this best.

Penetration of toothpastes, soaps, shampoos and so on are nearly 100 per cent in all Western countries and most of the more affluent Southeast Asian countries, as well as middle and upper income group households in many less affluent countries.

So would the penetration of white and brown goods such as TVs, laptops, mobile phones, microwave ovens and other kitchen gadgets, A/Cs, heating systems and so on be equally high. The growth in these markets is determined by 'replacement' needs, and the major players can only hope to accelerate the replacement cycle by introducing newer features in their products.

But in many geographies in Asia, Africa and Latin America, most of the above-mentioned products are either in the nascent or growth stage, giving many MNCs renewed opportunities.

Fortunately, in India, very few product categories, including mobile phones, have reached high enough penetration levels, in all geographies, income brackets, lifestyle segments and other differentiators to be termed as 'mature' markets. By default, therefore, all markets, barring the nascent category, are growth markets.

GROWTH MARKETS

Growth markets pose different challenges from 'mature' and 'nascent' markets.

While the first mover(s) is busy defending its position, early imitators focus on filling up product line, distribution and usage gaps. Such markets are most exposed to threats from new entrants and product substitutes, looking for niches to begin with, hoping to make it big soon.

Expecting a successful turnaround of an under-achieving company in such markets is therefore more realistic, as it would be fair to assume that the company, whichever industry it serves, would have some capabilities and even physical assets appropriate for such markets (having been in it in the first place) to adopt an asset-based turnaround strategy.

Strategy Options for Under-achieving Companies

Surprising as it may sound, there are many start-up companies which have under-performed not only in sunrise industries, but also in buoyant markets with high rates of growth. This is more apparent in companies not in control of their destinies, meaning they are not producing products for the end user.

Duracell had to recently close an alkaline battery manufacturing facility in India and transfer the machinery to another site in another country.

Duracell's demand is entirely device-led, meaning there is no use of a battery unless it is inside a device be it a toy, a flashlight, a laptop, a mobile phone or a pager. Duracell spotted an opportunity for their high-end batteries for pagers in India, an anticipated nascent market segment promising a longish window of opportunity, before mobile phones made their appearance, as it did in all other countries.

This turned out to be a 'ghost potential' as 'pagers' life was snuffed out early, owing to an almost simultaneous launch of mobile phones in the country.

Growth markets has created illusions of 'potential' in many other markets attracting different entrepreneurs, in different parts of India, to rush into filling up a perceived vacuum, unaware of each other's plans, and the result is a glut in a market of chronic 'shortages' created by a licensed regimen.

The result has been an underestimation of the funds that need to be employed and under-capitalization. Technologies have been chosen without enough attention to the company's readiness for absorbing such technology and equipment installed without adequate training for the operators. Bank borrowings have been heavy, and quite a few of these are now non-performing assets in bank books.

A turnaround CEO's task in such scenarios is to scout around for untenanted niches in the market which can be exploited.

Niche marketing requires careful segmentation of the present market construct and identification of the openings most easily exploited with current strengths, assets and capabilities.

Segmentation

The segmentation differentiators can be many ranging from geographies, product features, price, distribution, quality, reliability, after markets, to advertising, target audience profile and local myths.

GEOGRAPHIC SEGMENTATION

In most markets, competition is the strongest in the bigger cities and its suburbs. This is certainly true for consumer products, but also often true for intermediates as both the buyers'—direct and intermediaries—and sellers' offices tend to be located in such cities. However, in all developing economies, these boundaries are constantly changing, with potential buyers emerging in areas where the development benefits are reaching out for the first time.

In India, for example, there are a large number of Tier 1, 2, 3 and 4 cities followed by thousands of villages.

Over the years, a number of factors have significantly changed the lives of customers in such 'secondary' markets, resulting in higher levels of awareness, affluence and aspirations triggering off demands for products that had remained unstated and unsated. Simultaneously, better transport and communication facilities have made these geographies more accessible.

The sophistication levels in the secondary markets, as yet, are behind the bigger cities and many of the products driven out of the city markets have found a new life cycle in these markets. When the city homes are switching to gas-cooking ranges, a village home is graduating from wood to kerosene stoves. When a city home is buying flat back 42-inch colour TV, the village home is discovering black and white TVs. When a city home is buying longer lasting alkaline batteries, the village home is discovering paper clad batteries.

In effect, almost all products and markets are starting a fresh life cycle. The major players in the mature markets are aware of these opportunities. However, the extra effort and cost to tap these new markets are not always compatible with a milking strategy that dictates concentration on existing market segments.

The turnaround manager has an opportunity to find a competitive advantage as a virtual pioneer or a first mover in these geographies.

PRICE SEGMENTATION

All markets including commodities have different price bands.

Competing on price for the low end of the market is an immediate attraction for the turnaround manager. While it is true, that both in mature and growing markets, price can be an effective tool to gain market share, the turnaround manager needs to realize that such a strategy is not sustainable unless supported by low-cost capabilities.

If the turnaround manager wants to tap the market potential with price as the differentiator, he then has to direct his energies on building low-cost capabilities which will be the sum total of a number of initiatives in many operational areas. He will also have to be aware, that unless he is able to take some unique initiatives, the cost advantages will be short-lived as competitors will soon imitate and better such capabilities.

Low-cost Contributors

A direct approach to low cost is to pare the product down to its functional minimum as budget airlines have done in all markets, some profitably. In mature markets, it is fair to assume that the major players would have removed most of the frills as dictated by the milking strategy, and the turnaround manager will have few opportunities for further paring.

Even then innovation can play a role. A fringe player in the hair shampoo market, Velvette, unable to compete with Levers and Colgate, launched a single use sachet at a low unit price, thus dramatically accelerating the growth in the market. Velvette could savour its success only for a brief while, as the majors soon followed with sachets of their own.

Product Quality

The approach to product quality has to vary to match the needs of the business. A pioneer bringing in a revolutionary new product in the market may get away with some quality problems in its early days as the product concept effectively persuades the consumer to overlook these problems.

Companies which come later, as 'improvers' have to come in with better quality products to be able to get any share at all, often supported by add-on services such as installation and free annual maintenance contracts to make a sale.

A me-too product competes on price and is unlikely to have the quality standards of the improver or even the pioneer. It appeals to those segments unable to afford or unwilling to pay for the product standards set by the manufactures.

An under-achieving company's product may in very few cases be of considerably high quality and therefore unable to compete owing to the resultant high price.

This is an opportunity for the turnaround CEO to find an under-served premium niche and reposition his company's product for this niche only and to remember that only continuous product improvements will justify this positioning in the long run.

Process Economies

A turnaround CEO must also explore process economies to offer the customer better value for money. Bicycle manufacturers in India provide a good example of process economies.

The cycle manufacturers have created virtual factories in their dealers' premises. All cycle parts are delivered directly to the dealer by the vendors. A mechanic trained and armed with the correct tools quickly assembles a cycle for the customer, while he is having a cup of chai, as per the customer's specifications—mass 'customization' as the customer can decide on the product frills such as a racing handle, a bright red saddle or strapped pedals that he wants to add on.

The savings on labour, packaging, transport and transport damage are significant, some of which can be passed on to the customer.

Product Line Focus

Significant opportunities for improving efficiencies and profitability exist in streamlining the company's product range. It can be a significant contributor to building up low-cost capabilities.

Examples abound.

Some years ago, Chrysler embarked on a de-proliferation programme, by dropping 50 truck models, reducing engine combinations for the car lines to 75 from 179 and slashing axle selections to 68 from 142.

Similarly, the dashboard cluster choices for the Camaro were reduced to 96 from a mind-boggling 272 possible alternatives.

The de-proliferation programme had a negligible impact on sales, but made the manufacturing process less complicated, quality and efficiency in delivery improved and inventories slashed. Above all, the dealers found it easier to stock and sell a more manageable range of cars, trucks and optional extras and were ecstatic.

Textile mills, fashion and fashion accessory businesses have found similar benefits in reducing the product range. Paint companies have simplified inventories by introducing stainers that can be used in combination with standard foundation enamels.

LOW-SHARE STRATEGIES

Aiming for a low share of the market can at times be a very effective strategy. As the company positions itself for a small fringe of the market, it avoids the attention of the bigger players and is often able to command a price premium by offering specialty products. The difference between a niche and a low-share strategy is that while a company looks for an untenanted position in the market for a viable niche, the low-share strategy operates in the mainstream market but looks for differentials on an incremental basis.

Sensodyne, a gum disorder toothpaste, got a second wind in its sails when GSK brought its marketing and distribution skills in promoting OTC products to push Sensodyne to a wider audience. Sensodyne today is highly profitable brand in an otherwise cutthroat market dominated by P&G, Colgate and Levers.

Project engineering firms have used this strategy effectively in a number of market segments by focusing on small contracts and have at times benefited from receiving subcontracts from large competitors.

GROWTH STRATEGIES

There are many more strategies available to the turnaround CEO for the short and medium term.

The CEO must however remember that a company cannot be said to have successfully turned around if it merely stops making losses, and the creditors are temporarily off its back. If during the process of its turnaround it fails to restructure itself into a well-knit focused operation that can grow, to become a major player in its field of activity, it runs the risk of slipping down the ladder, and falling into hard times again at the emergence of the first symptoms of discontinuity.

The short-term strategy focus is confined to the immediate tasks, that is, to revitalize some part of the existing business with a view to stop cash losses and get the organization geared to improving operational efficiencies to create sustainable competitive advantages in a competitive world.

Growth Is the Turnaround Index

The long-term strategy focus has to shift to growth, and the turnaround manager's challenge is to find a market niche that provides the opportunity to grow.

Growth or the ability to grow must remain an important yardstick to measure the success of the turnaround strategy. Growth drives the principal business objectives of shareholder wealth, competitive sustainability and organizational vitality. Capital-efficient, profitable growth is the number one driver of shareholder value over periods of time.

That apart, growth has also been called pure oxygen.

'It creates a vital, enthusiastic corporation, where people see genuine opportunities. They take bigger chances, they work harder and smarter. In that way, growth is more than our single most important financial driver; it is an essential part of our corporate culture' says Wayne Calloway, the former CEO of PepsiCo in its annual report, when he stepped down.

Andrew Grant adds that a company has to earn 'the right to grow' and the one of the key steps in preparing to grow lies in the superior operational performance. It is important to make sure that the existing businesses are operating well and their fundamentals are in good shape.

Without growth, many a turnaround would end up as an illusion.

Growth Options

Evaluating growth markets independent of the company's capabilities or the core competencies is futile. The colour TV market in China and India is growing very rapidly. It certainly provides an opportunity to Sony, but it is of little relevance to Unilever or Proctor & Gamble. The Internet has opened up new frontiers and a number of companies have struck it very rich very quickly. While the Internet can be an important new channel for sales, an engineering company specializing in the manufacture of heavy machinery is unlikely to be able to use its assets in running a portal.

But the choice of the market is important. It should be of fair size, registering a reasonable year-on-year volume growth. It shouldn't have a behemoth controlling 70–80 per cent share. Whereas a new company can rewrite the rules in an established market, an under-performing company with its carry forward baggage, will not be able to. Neither should the market be fragmented, with low-entry barriers, to make the company's products vulnerable to both low price and innovative competition.

And ideally, the market should not be dependent on a series of ifs and when's, such as waiting for government expenditure to pick up or regulatory controls to be lifted.

Companies that have prospered over a period of time tend to look at opportunities adjacent to their business largely because a company's capabilities are generally more suitable for moving up or down the value-added chain in the industry it has been operating in. A pharmaceutical intermediary manufacture, for example, can either move a step backwards to make the chemicals required in the manufacture of the intermediate or move forward to making formulations.

The turnaround manager has to therefore look at the related opportunities to decide on the long-term strategy for the company.

Backward Integration

Backward integration is best avoided as it ties the company down to its current business and limits its flexibility if new technologies change the market or product delivery systems.

That apart, backward integration normally requires large investments in technology, equipment and plant, resources that the early stages of turnaround may not generate unless the company uses input items that are produced in low-tech plants. In such cases, the process tends to be manpower intensive. Entry into such industries requires careful consideration.

Manpower costs can be deceptive. In a developing country, even if the wages of a worker are as little as US$ 2,000 in the first year, the company will end up spending over US$ 450,000 on such a worker, when all the increments, bonuses, medical insurance, social security, leave pay and training costs are computed over his normal working career of 30 years. Hiring one extra worker becomes actually equivalent to clearing a capital investment of close to US$ 100,000, on a discounted cash flow basis, assuming inflation at 5 per cent per annum.

A company should therefore deliberate on hiring additional manpower with as much diligence as it applies to a large capital item purchase. Unfortunately, this rarely happens. Many companies, especially under-performing companies, often end up with surplus manpower, primarily because the long-term ramifications have been overlooked when opting for a manpower intensive process in preference to an automated process. The argument often is lack of funds for capital outlay or absence of automated technology at the point of time such recruitments took place. Had the management been alert to the need of continuous review of manning norms, especially with the introduction of relevant new technologies, distress may have been avoided.

A turnaround manager cannot therefore really consider backward integration into manpower intensive manufacturing processes as a long-term strategy.

However, such backward integration may be useful if a turnaround manager inherits a large under-utilized workforce that cannot be reduced owing to environmental pressures. He may then like to do so as a tactical measure, but *only for the very short term*.

Forward Integration

Increasing profitability by taking a product further up the value chain is always an attractive proposition for a turnaround CEO.

Moving up the value chain to get close to the end consumer normally would require development of marketing skills, an infrastructure to tap new distribution channels and resources to build brand equity. Such a strategy also needs to address the impact on the relationship with current customers, as forward integration may result in head-to-head competition with present buyers of the company's products.

Fabric manufacturers have found making garments a natural forward integration opportunity. Only few have succeeded, as garments not only require expertise in distribution and marketing, but also time to build a brand franchise. If existing customers stop buying fabric from a company threatening to be a future competitor, the fabric manufacture loses out on its bread and butter business and the consequent ability to support a branded line of goods.

It is better to forward integrate to enter markets where the company's present customers are not represented.

A supplier of chicken to say KFC develops the confidence to launch a range of frozen and processed chicken and pre-cooked chicken dishes for sale in supermarkets and own outlets by processing its products to the demanding standards of KFC, as Kingdom of Chicken has done successfully.

This will be a sound strategy as KFC is unlikely to enter the packaged frozen foods market and will continue to source its chicken from such a company.

The additional capabilities necessary to succeed with a forward integration strategy can be built over time as Amul has done in India.

Amul is the brand name of a premium range of dairy products marketed by a dairy farmer co-operative that was set up in the Kaira district of Gujarat in the 1950s. The purpose of this co-operative was to collect milk from individual farmers, all of whom had become shareholders of the co-operative, and supply fresh milk to the city of Mumbai, some 400 kilometres away. Mumbai was a fast-growing city and the demand for milk was high.

The co-operative in due course set up advisory services to help farmers adopt better animal husbandry processes, and harvest better milk yields. Additionally, with new members joining the co-operative, attracted by the benefits of collective marketing, the co-operative's daily collection of milk was increasing faster than the demand for fresh milk.

This put pressure on the co-operative to find ways and means to preserve unsold milk. It started processing milk powders, butter and *ghee*, a popular cooking medium in India, with the Amul brand name, in the first phase. The technology was fairly simple and the production facilities were by now affordable. Despite being on virtually the first rung of the value chain, these products ensured a higher return per litre of milk, a fact greatly appreciated by its members.

As the co-operative gained experience in marketing and distributing packaged and branded products, it was encouraged to explore avenues for greater value addition. Today it also markets baby formulations, cheese, ice creams, chocolates and milk-based desserts, all of which are competing successfully with multinational giants such as Nestle.

Amul's forward integration ventures have succeeded for a number of reasons—consistently high quality, reasonable prices, good advertising and effective distribution. Not having to compete head on with a current customer of its basic product, liquid milk helped, as its present income was never under threat.

Sustainable Growth Essentials

The turnaround CEO must take a leaf out of Amul's book and build three essential pillars of sustainable growth for a long period of time, which are *brand, patents and IP.*

If any of these three are absent in a company, then that company will remain vulnerable to market swings and remain a turn-around prospect sooner than later.

Setting up R&D labs, registering and protecting trademarks, patenting formulations and processes take time and money. When the day-to-day pressures for survival diminish, the CEO must engage outside consultants to ensure availability of adequate funds to build the three essentials.

Finding Resources for Long-term Viability

The profits generated from the operations of a company coming out of the stresses of a turnaround will not be enough to build the three essentials—brand, patents and IP.

Additional resources will be required to buy new technology, upgrade production facilities, invest in R&D, develop new skills, add critical mass through acquisitions, exit irrelevant businesses, the list will be endless.

The options available to raise funds will not be too many. Expanding the equity base, attractive on paper, is rarely feasible, as present shareholders are unlikely to respond to a rights issue and new shareholders will not buy into an under-performing company.

New loans will have to be negotiated from the current lenders.

Lenders have high stakes in the company as well, and it is in nobody's interest to see a company go down under, for lack of funds.

The lenders will however want to see a sound business plan. But more than that, they will need convincing that the management is not only able but also committed to succeed. The turnaround manager will have to exude confidence in himself and his team and it helps, if he carries his passion for the business on his sleeve.

EPILOGUE

A Few Years Later

I t was a bright sunny morning when the C-Suite trooped in, all relaxed in casual clothes, to the CEO's office, responding to an e-mail requesting a meeting, but for once without an agenda.

Good morning, everyone, said the finance director, looking at the CEO. We meet without an agenda and that too at a short notice. Has something happened? Is there a new crisis looming on the horizon?

The marketing director, equally intrigued, says there can't be. Orders are flowing in steadily; customers are happy getting delivery on time. And would you believe it? I haven't seen or heard of a single quality complaint in the last six months.

The director manufacturing chips in, why should you? Our capacity-building plans were completed ahead of the schedule. All the machines are purring away smoothly, there is no downtime. Absenteeism is no longer an issue, and the factories are running at full capacity.

VP, HRD says, give us some credit for that. The unions are fully behind our zero tolerance for defects programme. That apart, they are asking for more skill development programmes across the board.

The director of supply chain says my only problem now is that, I don't have enough time on my hands to accept all the lunch and dinner invites from the CEOs of all our vendors...

Lucky you, interrupts the finance director. Then where is the crisis?

The CEO looks around the table, nods at everyone, and says, yes, everything seems to be going well. I must compliment you all.

Some questions bother me though. Where would our future growth come from?

What are our competitors up to? They must be streamlining their operations as well. Are our customers planning on migrating to new technologies? Will our products remain relevant to them? How many disruptors are quietly working on substitutes which may soon rain on our parade? We need to go in for more automation. Should we invest on the same technology or look for new technology partners? Would the union support us? Are the economic trends favourable to us?

I think it's time for us to agree on our next goal. How about doubling our sales and profits every two years? How about making our present topline our bottom line in four years? Can we do that if we remain in the same business?

I propose a two-day retreat to mull over these and invite some strategy and domain experts to make us more sensitive to the emerging business environment. Any suggestions?

INDEX

ABOUT THE AUTHOR

Pradip Chanda is a management consultant, author, columnist and noted speaker on the subject of corporate turnarounds and start-ups.

During a corporate career lasting more than 40 years, including 20 as a CEO, Pradip's core competency has been the ability to conceptualize and champion clear business strategies while maintaining focus on achieving operational results.

Following graduation from Calcutta University, Pradip began his working career as a management trainee at Hindustan Unilever Ltd, Bombay in 1966. He spent the next 19 years holding senior management positions in marketing and new product development with Unilever and GlaxoSmithKline, based in Bombay, Delhi and London.

In 1985, Pradip shifted to the entertainment industry as president and CEO of Gramophone Co. of India Ltd, better known as HMV. HMV's turnaround, from the verge of closure to its re-emergence as the #1 music company in India, is perhaps the most successful restructuring case in India of its time.

While, at HMV, Pradip made a significant contribution in steering the adoption of an internationally acceptable IP protection regime for entertainment software in India, and setting up anti-piracy initiatives as the president of Indian Phonographic Industry (1986–93), an affiliate of IFPI (International Federation of Phonographic Industries).

Since 2002 Pradip has worn a number of different hats—author, business strategy consultant, professor, mentor to three start-ups in media, entertainment and technology.

Previous Books

The Second Coming: Creativity in Corporate Turnarounds (Tata McGraw-Hill, Delhi 2000).

The international edition titled *Corporate Turnaround: Strategies for Renewal* marketed globally (McGraw Hill, SG).

A Requiem for a Brand (Roli Books 2010) takes a provocative look at the changing face of global marketing.